YOU ARE LOVED!!

How God Longs to Empower You!

JENNIFER KIYONAGA

10-10-10
Publishing

ISBN: 978-1-77277-073-5

PUBLISHER
10-10-10 PUBLISHING
MARKHAM, ON
CANADA

DEDICATION

I dedicate this book to my late husband,
Richard Kiyonaga
and our wonderful family:
Tomiko and Greg,
Kiyomi and Orest,
Hudson,
and my dear, delightful grandchildren,
Asher, Caleb, Lev and Liliana.

I love you dearly and you bless me every day!
Love Mom, Nana, and MIL

Cherish your visions and your dreams, as they are the children of your soul, the blueprints of your ultimate achievements.

—Napoleon Hill, author, 1883-1970

TABLE OF CONTENTS

ACKNOWLEDGEMENTS

My family: Thank you for loving me as you do. You fill my heart with pride, joy and love. I am so blessed and very grateful that I have such a wonderful loving family.

Raymond Aaron: Thank you for your passion to teach people to author a book. It has been one of the hardest things I have done, but definitely one of the most rewarding. You are the **REAL** deal.

Steven Pressfield: Thank you for so graciously giving me permission to quote your very insightful book, *The War of Art.* Your immediate, positive response of, "Quote away" to my e-mail was so exciting and encouraging. It was my first "pinch me" moment in writing my book.

Cara Witvoet: You were amazing in your faithful encouragement to get my book done. Your kind, affirming support just made the process so much easier and exciting! We did it! I now think of you as my book's midwife!

Karen Maier: Thank you for assisting in the editing of this book. You are a born editor and a dear and faithful friend. I am blessed to have you in my life.

Marina Wieland: You are the kindest, most generous, supportive friend anyone could ask for. Thank you for helping me with the book in so many ways: for suggesting the last chapter format, helping me with the editing, bringing me food, and most of all, for being my prayer partner every day. You bless me daily.

Connie Garvey: Thank You for being so thrilled, supportive, and proud of my book! Your prayers meant a lot to me. You are my one of a kind, dear friend who brings me joy whenever we can be together!

Bob Proctor and Sandy Gallagher: Thank you, Bob Proctor, for opening my eyes to see the unseen, and thank you, Sandy Gallagher, for believing in me.

Doris Schuster: I am so grateful to have found your company ChristianEditingServices.org Thank you for your Assistance.

Jesus Christ, Yeshua HaMashiach: You are my Lord, my Saviour, and the co-author of this book. My gratitude is endless for all of the blessings I have in you.

FOREWORD

Jennifer Kiyonaga's previous career as a registered nurse has given her years of experience in counselling, comforting, and providing inspiration to many. She has taken the ability to provide comfort and inspiration that she had for her patients, and channelled it into this book, in order to do the same for you.

You Are Loved!! is a book about the power that has always been within you, and is always readily available to you. The power is Universal Energy and Spirit which is everywhere present at all times. Jennifer teaches you that you are seamlessly connected to this Universal Energy. If there is anything that you have dreamed of or desired, this book will give you the key to understanding. *You Are Loved!!* will help you to believe in yourself and will allow you to attain more than you ever thought possible. Alexander Graham Bell said, "What this power is I cannot say: all I know is that it exists." I recommend that you read this book, get inspired and take enthusiastic action in your life. When you believe in your dream, there is no limit to how far you can go.

This book is written from Jennifer's Christian perspective, but is meant to be relevant to you so that you can find and achieve more in your own life.

—**Raymond Aaron**
   New York Times Bestselling Author

INTRODUCTION

It is no coincidence that you have picked up this book, because it was meant for you. I know this, for when I was about to write this book, I knelt in prayer and asked God to allow its message to find those who were to read it. So please know that I have thought of you, prayed for you and even imagined how the book came to be in your hands. I am wondering if you are in a bookstore, a trade show, a seminar, a doctor's office, or if it has been given to you as a gift. It is my story of feeling lost, and then being found by God. Having been on a long adventure with God, I know how much He longs for you to know Him and how much He wants to be a part of your life. God will never impose on you, but will wait till you are ready to share your life with Him.

So come along and listen, not only to my story, but to the very words of the ancient book that was inspired by the Spirit of God. This book will let you peer into the window of wisdom that comes from God. You will learn secrets that will allow you to unlock power that is from on high and learn ways to transform your life, because you are loved!

Chapter 1

LOST BUT NOW FOUND

You are loved! This I know, for the Bible tells me so. The Bible is the book of ancient wisdom which was written over a period of 1500 years. It was written by over forty people who were inspired by God. The writers included shepherds, fishermen, priests, a physician, kings and prophets. The Bible was the first book ever printed when Gutenberg invented the printing press in 1454 A.D, and has been a perennial best seller ever since. It is a book that is banned in many countries with the penalty for possession being death or imprisonment.

In the countries where it is outlawed, people risk their lives to possess a copy, and others risk theirs by smuggling Bibles to those hoping to own one. Many have gone to the far reaches of the earth to live among unknown people groups and tribes to share the deep wisdom that is contained within it. They leave everything familiar and dear to them to travel far from home, and learn a foreign language, in order to share its message of LOVE. It is a book that is not allowed in schools, but is welcomed in prisons. It is a book that keeps its secrets from those who would read it without a sincere heart. The Bible is no ordinary book, and it will remain a mystery to those who approach it from a purely intellectual standpoint. It is a spiritual book, inspired by the Holy Spirit, and will reveal its deep truths only to those who come truly seeking to find God.

1 Corinthians 2:14

The person without the Spirit does not accept the things that come from the Spirit of God but considers them foolishness, and cannot understand them because they are discerned only through the Spirit.

It is evident that the Word will remain a mystery unless the inner secrets are discerned with the help of supernatural forces. If the Bible is just a book to you, and you wish to add it to the list of books that you have read, then that is what it will remain: just another ordinary book. I have heard many people say they have read the Bible. I would comment: "Yes, you may have read it; but has it spoken to you?" Early in Scriptures, it states, "You will seek me and find me when you seek me with all your heart." (Jeremiah 29:13) Who is the *me* in that statement? That statement is from the very heart of God.

It was almost forty years ago that I went searching for God with my whole heart. The ancient Scriptures have become my best friend and the book without which I would be so very lost. It is the book that has comforted me in my deepest sorrows and greatest challenges. It has brought me to tears, and still does, by the great, loving heart of God, who longs to be known and loved in return. I was not always respectful of God or His message to me, so let me share a bit of my story. It is a story of rebellion and disdain that turned into a search for something that seemed to call to me from within.

I was very rebellious when I was young. I left home in my teens and soon spiralled downward in the drug-hazed days of the 60s. My dear mother had no idea what had become of me or where I was. My mom would lay awake at night and hope I was alive and doing well. I never contacted her. To her, I was lost out there in the world somewhere. She called the police, but they said there was nothing they could do since I was older than 16. She began to make an almost nightly call to a night shift police sergeant who would listen to her and encourage her as best he could. I am sure she prayed, but it would be years before her faith would be the anchor of her life. As a mother and a grandmother now, I cannot imagine the inner suffering and worry that I caused my own mother.

While she sat alone in her apartment, I was out on some drug-hazed, speed-fuelled run. As time went on, and I did more and more drugs, my health deteriorated and my mind became lost in confusion and delirium. I became increasingly paranoid. I do believe that the paranoia actually saved my life, and it was in some drug-fuelled state that I eventually called my brother-in-law to come and get me. I had a copy of a section of the local newspaper that clarified a conspiracy to me. I knew that I had to leave as soon as possible.

My brother-in-law came with the police, and they collected me and my meagre belongings. I shared the newspaper article with them, telling them it would explain everything. It was an article about some politicians.

As my brother-in-law drove, I crouched on the floor, overcome with fear. I think he was uneasy, not knowing if what I was experiencing had any truth to it. We arrived at my sister's place and I remember they were very concerned for my well-being. The newspaper article revealed nothing to them and I could not explain it to them.

I was taken to my mother's home, thin, weak, and wired with fear and anxiety. I weighed about eighty pounds. I had not eaten or slept for days and was fearful to be in my mother's apartment. I stayed on the balcony and was too afraid to go inside. My mother convinced me to see the doctor who prescribed a sedative, and then I slept. Feeling groggy when I awoke, I really did not know what was before me or what I was to do next in my life.

My mother and sister agreed that I should go to 999 Queen Street for treatment. 999 Queen had always struck fear in me. It was Toronto's notorious, ancient insane asylum. It was a large old building, blackened with age. A thick, high wall of the same blackened brick surrounded the grounds. It always seemed more prison-like to me than a place of healing and help. So many shadowy stories existed of the misunderstood treatments provided within its dark, dirty walls. The building was huge, walled, and imposing. There was nothing friendly or inviting about it. I was very uneasy about going there, but realized that I had to do something to find my equilibrium in life. So I agreed to go.

I remember driving to the old insane asylum with my mother and sister. As we drove, the collective anxiety of the three of us hung heavy in the air. We drove up and I wondered what I was going to experience in this battered old building. Check-in seemed normal enough, with pleasant offices and admitting staff. However, when I was taken to the ward, I was deeply disturbed by what I saw. We entered a dim, spiral staircase with brick walls that twisted its way to the ward. I was unsettled by the huge ring of old keys clutched in the nurse's hands. It reminded me of some old black and white movie I may have seen when I was younger.

I was becoming increasingly nervous and I could feel the same growing concern in my mother and sister. We entered the ward. It was a huge, empty space. The halls were wide and high, and devoid of any furniture that I can remember. I was taken to a large room with about eight iron, beat-up cots with chipped, white paint. The lights were bright and harsh; the bed coverings plain and thin. Five women lay on their beds, staring at the blank ceiling.

When I was taken into the middle of the room, the nurse announced to everyone in the room, "Now, we have Jennifer." One woman sat bolt upright and loudly proclaimed, "Jennifer!" I was young and troubled, but I was not like these women. It seemed like their very lifeblood was drained from their faces, which were blank and pale like the bedding. My mind had rested enough to let me know that I did not want to be there. My mind raced, wondering if it was too late. Would they make me stay? My heart pounded within my chest.

The nurse turned to me and told me to go and put my pyjamas

on. I told her it was 4:00 p.m. in the afternoon and I was not going to do that. I looked toward my mom and told her that I did not want to stay, not then, not ever. My mom and sister were dismayed, but in their eyes, I could see that they felt just as uncomfortable as I did about leaving me in that place. The nurse eyed me and my family, and tried to convince us that it would be the best for me. My anxiety heightened. It was with great relief when the nurse told us that this was a voluntary admission, and there was nothing to keep me. I was free to go! My chest expanded in a big sigh of relief. I can still hear the clinking of the large, old keys as I made my way down the dark, claustrophobic, twisting stairs till I felt the warmth of the sun and fresh air fill my lungs. The oppressive heaviness of the deadness of that ward was gone. My mom and sister felt challenged at deciding what to do next. I returned to my mom's apartment and spent the next few weeks eating, sleeping, and slowly healing my mind and body.

One morning, at a loss of how best to help me, my mom handed me a book on Christianity. At first I did not know what the book was about, but when I discovered what the subject was, I slapped the book shut and threw it across the room. I had nothing but disdain for anything to do with religion. I had grown up with my father's religion of Christian Science, which had been a source of anger between my mother and father. This religion believed that illness was in the mind and did not encourage seeking medical assistance. As a young teen, I had heard on the radio that there was an inquest into the death of a baby from pneumonia. The parents had not sought medical intervention because of their religion. I was angered that a baby died and therefore rejected religion at that young, impressionable age.

Soon afterwards, I regained my strength, but my mind was plagued with paralyzing bouts of anxiety in social settings. Sometimes the emptiness in my soul was so consummate that the void felt like a black, yawning abyss. I wondered what I was going to do with my life, but eventually I found a job as a waitress. After several years of working at varying jobs, I entered college. I switched programs a couple of times and then settled on Nursing. I completed the nursing program and became a registered nurse. It must have been something of a miracle to my mother. My life took on a sense of normalcy. I was a nurse, I had a good job, and I had friends from the Nursing program and also at work. Weekends were spent partying, having a good time, and then "nursing" hangover after hangover!

I met the man of my dreams, and everybody else's from what I have heard. Richard was kind, loving, steady, handsome, and just the nicest person you could meet. I was still shaky with my anxiety and moods, and was falling apart before my wedding day. I called the Clark Institute, a psychiatric facility in Toronto, and told them I was getting married in three weeks. I told them they had two weeks to help me get it together. They admitted me to a day program for those two weeks and they interviewed Richard without me. I was terrified that he would postpone or cancel the wedding. However, his love stood firm, and he steadied me, stood by me, and married me just one week after being released from the Clark Crisis Intervention program. I really do not know what would have become of me if he had thought our relationship was too fraught with emotional challenges to risk a lifetime for it. I do know that I would have been devastated.

I was happily married and loved. Everything looked normal from the outside. Richard felt life was just fine and we were content, even if my emotional ups and downs were somewhat of a challenge. He was good at riding the emotional waves with me and was the rock and anchor I needed in my life. I remember wondering why a pervasive feeling that something was missing persisted. What more could there be? Shiny objects and new possessions did not call to me; they were never the things that I seemed to need or want. Yet there was a void that I just could not shush or fill.

One day, I had the revelation that the emptiness was spiritual in nature, so I purchased a Bible and a booklet called *Proverbs*. Every day I read one of the chapters of Proverbs to Richard. I was struck by the repeating theme to "seek knowledge, gain wisdom and get understanding." Proverbs 2:2-3 tells us to turn our ear to wisdom, apply our heart to understanding, call out for insight, cry aloud for understanding, and then it says to look and search for these things like silver or like hidden treasure. It goes on to say that only after this deep searching and asking will we find the knowledge of God who gives wisdom, and understanding. The theme was repeated over and over as I read.

I would ask Richard, "What is it that we are to know? What are we to understand? What is the wisdom that this book is speaking of?" All I had ever heard about religion was to have faith and believe. That seemed simple enough. My heart compelled me to find the answer to this riddle which puzzled my heart and soul. What was my soul searching for?

I began a church search on Sundays. Every Sunday I would drag Richard to a different church denomination. We searched throughout the city, but I just could not find the answer for my questioning heart. My husband graciously accompanied me and I remember finally coming to the conclusion that I did not know what I was searching for. I thought it must be craziness in my mind, so I stopped searching. My mother would tell me to go to the local Baptist church in our community. I remember telling her that "I would never become a holy roller, Bible-thumping Baptist!" Although I was not too sure what that statement meant, I had heard it said of Baptists, and I was not going to become one of them!

One Sunday was very different. Richard and I had spent the afternoon watching a football game. We had leisurely read through the newspaper which lay strewn all about. We had snacked our way through the day. It was a quiet and restful afternoon, and we were relaxed and content. I began to feel a prompting to shower and change, and go to the evening service at the very Baptist church that I did not want to go to. I felt I was supposed to go alone and not ask Richard to join me. This was very odd because we did everything together. He looked up and asked me what I was doing. I told him I was going to church and I knew that, if I asked him to come with me, he would say, "No," and that would be enough to influence me and keep me from going. Instead, he just said, "Ok, good-bye." I thought of taking my unread Bible, but was too embarrassed to carry it outdoors. I am a person who drives everywhere. However, that evening I did not take the car, but began to walk. It was quite a distance for me. I felt peaceful and calm. As I walked, I looked at the houses, the gardens and the trees that I passed. The sense that I was being led by something filled me with quietness and deep peace within my soul.

I entered the church and found a seat in the old, heavy, curved pews of the circular shaped sanctuary. The service started with old hymns and announcements and, although my mind may have wandered, something expectant seemed to fill me. What was I doing here and why was I here on this Sunday evening? The pastor began his sermon and I listened to his every word. He began to preach that Jesus had died for us on the cross to pay the death penalty for all the sin in the world. He said that it was a gift to be received or rejected. The pastor then stated that the longer we reject Jesus, the harder it becomes to accept the gift of forgiveness from God. He also said that our rejection wounded the very heart of God. I instinctively sensed this was it! This was what I was to know and understand from Proverbs. The light bulb went on in my mind and the wisdom of it called aloud to me.

The pastor then asked everyone to bow their heads and close their eyes. He asked if there were any who would like to begin the Christian life to please put up their hand. Suddenly, a force descended upon me and I was engulfed in an inner battle. My face became flushed and I felt a surge of energy charge through me. My heart pounded within my chest, and the palms of my hands perspired and became clammy and cold. Part of me was saying "Put up your hand!" but the other part of me countered, "Do not put up your hand!" This intense battle raged back and forth within my mind and manifested in the physical. My whole being was at war and I could not move. The pastor kept saying, "We will wait a little while longer," as the battle continued within me. When the invitation ended, the duality of the inner struggle did not stop. I had not put up my hand and I felt like I had made the supreme rejection mixed with sadness. The other part of me just felt a sense of relief, almost akin to something like, "Phew that was close!" I felt quite shaken by what I had experienced. Finally, the pastor said, "If you did not put up your hand, please come and talk with me on the way out of the church."

As the congregation made its way to the door, everyone shook the hand of the pastor. When I reached him, I shared what had happened to me during the service. He looked into my eyes and told me that the Holy Spirit had come upon me and that is why I had encountered such a strange experience. The pastor asked me to come to his office and spend a moment with him in prayer. We entered his book-filled, softly-lit office and he began to explain to me what had happened. He said that God had brought me there that day. I remember feeling that whatever had been upon me was gone. I told him that I would come back sometime in the week to discuss it. He impressed upon me the importance of praying a short prayer even though the battle within had subsided. The pastor led me to pray a simple prayer. He would say a few words and I would repeat the words. I am not going to share the prayer with you now, but you will find it later in this book.

I thanked the pastor and made my way home, feeling somewhat confused as I walked along. The peace that had accompanied me to the church was still there, but it had changed in some way. My thoughts were deep and meditative as I reflected on all that I had experienced within me in that church. Finally, I reached our building, and took the elevator to our floor. As I opened the door and looked at Richard sitting on the couch, he looked at me and proclaimed, "What happened to you tonight?"

I quietly responded, "I don't know." I did not understand it all but I knew that something had changed.

Let's just say that fateful night changed the course of my life. My spirit had been awakened to the things of the God whom I had rejected and disdained all my life. It would be nice to say that a magic wand had been waved over my life and I was completely new. However, it would be more accurate to say that I felt like I had been found by the Spirit of love that had come for me in my search for God. This Spirit led me to that church and fought for me, and I am so happy that He won the battle.

How I longed to get to the top of the ladder so I could be changed completely. I can honestly say it did not happen that way. I had to take one rung at a time, and often go back two and start again. A daily battle continued to try to defeat me in my quest for spiritual growth. My heart was captured and every time the door of the church opened, I wanted to be there. I remember going to a Bible study and thinking that the only reason the Lord came for me was that God really did not want me, but truly wanted my husband Richard to know and be known by Him. That was a sad revelation of my incredibly low self-esteem. I am innately a quitter in the challenges of life, but the love that purchased my pardon proved faithful over and over again, even when I was faithless.

Jeremiah 31:3

The Lord has appeared of old to me, saying:
"I have loved you with an everlasting love;
I have drawn you with unfailing kindness."

From that starting point, with such a low perception of my worth, the Lord and His Word eventually taught me to believe that I was truly loved. I had so much unlearning to do, so much drama to let go of, so much of me to release so that God could work His will in my life. Since my divine experience with God, I have been captivated by Jesus. My heart was captured with an energy that filled my soul with a hunger to know more. I was impassioned to share this newly-found relationship with everyone that I knew. My heart broke over and over again as people did not understand or accept what I was sharing. I had only raw, unstoppable enthusiasm to tell the story of this amazing LOVE that had taken my whole heart in a battle that had raged within it. I lived in dismay at the incredible indifference and the outright rejection for the things of faith.

My attempts to share my experience were met with disdain and indifference. It was everywhere. My family mocked me; my friends closed their ears and hearts to what I had to share. My husband was not interested. I was alone in my faith, except within the walls of my church. I now understood why the church was sometimes called the Holy Huddle. Our message was not welcome outside of the church walls. The message of "Holy, Redeeming Love" resonated with only a few.

I became quiet about my faith and spoke of it less and less. My Christian walk was still so far from what it should be. Though I thought my faith was weak and not of much worth, it was a time of growth and increasing sensitivity to the things of the Spirit and the Word. Unbeknownst to me, the Lord was slowly building me up in Him. He was validating my quietness about Him with the verse below:

1 Peter 3:15

But in your hearts revere Christ as Lord. Always be prepared to give an answer to everyone who asks you to give the reason for the hope that you have. But do this with gentleness and respect.

I love the tender heart of God that tells us to be prepared to answer, but to answer with gentleness and respect. He longs to be known, but will never force His love upon us. When I was a nurse, caring for the sick and dying, I distinctly heard a voice that said to me, "Rescue the perishing!" I saw so much fear experienced by my patients as the end of their life approached. In those times, when all hope was gone, their only comfort became my faith, which I would freely share with them. People who lived in total indifference to God, now clamoured for some hope in the midst of the darkness and the unknown that lay before them. The Lord always proved merciful and comforting. His love never fails.

I must admit that, over the years, my walk with the Lord has been a meandering path of ups and downs. Yet, one thing I can say is that He has stayed true to His Word and He has loved me with an everlasting love that has never failed me. God is Spirit and that Spirit is love. We cannot see or touch that Spirit, but the Spirit of God calls you His "treasured possession" in Deuteronomy 7:6. God repeats this lovely sentiment in several other Scriptures. We are His treasured possession! When was the last time someone told you that you were treasured? I can say I have never had anyone express their love with such devotion. Think of your children. They are treasured, valued and irreplaceable. You love them with your very life and they are treasured by you. God said that is how He feels about you! He longs to be gracious to you and show Himself strong on your behalf. He says that even the hairs on your head are counted. Isaiah 43:4 states that you are precious and honoured in His sight and that He loves you. King David, who was once a shepherd spent many a night looking deep into the vast heavens and endless expanse of sky. He questioned the Great Creator God:

Psalm 8:3-4

When I consider your heavens,
the work of your fingers,
the moon and the stars,
which you have set in place,
⁴ what is mankind that you are mindful of them,
human beings that you care for them?

These verses are comparing the magnitude of the heavens, the moon and the stars to mankind. Compared to the vastness of the universe, we are so small and insignificant. Even the earth, which is our home within the universe, is a tiny pinhead in the scheme of creation. Yet God is mindful of you. He knows the number of hairs on your head, and if you do not have any, He knows that too. God created you and He knows what you desire above all—and that is unfailing love. We have all known people who feel this void and find all kinds of ways to fill the God-shaped vacuum within them. They think possessions, shiny new toys, drugs, alcohol, infidelity or other empty forms of activity will fill the void. In many ways, these empty pursuits just make the seeker feel they need more and more to conquer the lack of fulfillment within. I know, because I have been there. My favourite Scripture is:

Isaiah 41:10

So do not fear, for I am with you;
do not be dismayed, for I am your God.
I will strengthen you and help you;
I will uphold you with my righteous right hand.

God is love and He cannot do anything but love you. He is a gentle God and, oh, how He longs to be your Abba Father. *Abba* is a familiar term much akin to Dad. The Bible says in 1 Corinthians 2:9 that "no eye has seen, no ear has heard what God has prepared for those who love Him." He longs to be loved just as much as you do. There is so much more I could share about His tender heart. It takes time to truly understand and know Him. In my relationship with God, much time has been spent in the ancient Scriptures. His mighty heart reveals itself to you in the Bible. Coming into contact with God's great heart is profoundly moving. To know the Almighty God who loves you, you must go to Him daily and seek to know His ways, precepts and truths. Then, slowly, the veil will lift from your eyes and you will come into contact with the very loving heart of God. There are many poignant verses about His sad heart. God sits on the sidelines of our lives and tries, over and over again, to get our attention.

Jeremiah 32:33
They turned their backs to me and not their faces; though I taught them again and again, they would not listen or respond to discipline.

Can you imagine how you would feel if, every time you spoke to your children, they turned their backs to you? Let me share something that a pastor was prompted to write based on Scripture. It is called "The Father's Love Letter," and is completely taken from the Holy Bible. Recorded versions of "The Father's Love Letter" can be found on YouTube.

My Child,

You may not know me,
but I know everything about you.
Psalm 139:1

I know when you sit down and when you rise up.
Psalm 139:2

I am familiar with all your ways.
Psalm 139:3

Even the very hairs on your head are numbered.
Matthew 10:29-31

For you were made in my image.
Genesis 1:27

In me you live and move and have your being.
Acts 17:28

For you are my offspring.
Acts 17:28

I knew you even before you were conceived.
Jeremiah 1:4-5

I chose you when I planned creation.
Ephesians 1:11-12

You were not a mistake,
for all your days are written in my book.
Psalm 139:15-16

I determined the exact time of your birth
and where you would live.
Acts 17:26

You are fearfully and wonderfully made.
Psalm 139:14

I knit you together in your mother's womb.
Psalm 139:13

And brought you forth on the day you were born.
Psalm 71:6

I have been misrepresented
by those who don't know me.
John 8:41-44

I am not distant and angry,
but am the complete expression of love.
1 John 4:16

And it is my desire to lavish my love on you.
1 John 3:1

Simply because you are my child
and I am your Father.
1 John 3:1

I offer you more than your earthly father
ever could.
Matthew 7:11

For I am the perfect father.
Matthew 5:48

Every good gift that you receive comes from my hand.
James 1:17

For I am your provider and I meet all your needs.
Matthew 6:31-33

My plan for your future has always been filled with hope.
Jeremiah 29:11

Because I love you with an everlasting love.
Jeremiah 31:3

My thoughts toward you are countless
as the sand on the seashore.
Psalms 139:17-18

And I rejoice over you with singing.
Zephaniah 3:17

I will never stop doing good to you.
Jeremiah 32:40

For you are my treasured possession.
Exodus 19:5

I desire to establish you
with all my heart and all my soul.
Jeremiah 32:41

And I want to show you great and marvelous things.
Jeremiah 33:3

If you seek me with all your heart,
you will find me.
Deuteronomy 4:29

Delight in me and I will give you
the desires of your heart.
Psalm 37:4

For it is I who gave you those desires.
Philippians 2:13

I am able to do more for you
than you could possibly imagine.
Ephesians 3:20

For I am your greatest encourager.
2 Thessalonians 2:16-17

I am also the Father who comforts you
in all your troubles.
2 Corinthians 1:3-4

When you are brokenhearted,
I am close to you.
Psalm 34:18

As a shepherd carries a lamb,
I have carried you close to my heart.
Isaiah 40:11

One day I will wipe away
every tear from your eyes.
Revelation 21:3-4

And I'll take away all the pain
you have suffered on this earth.
Revelation 21:3-4

I am your Father, and I love you
even as I love my son, Jesus.
John 17:23

For in Jesus, my love for you is revealed.
John 17:26

He is the exact representation of my being.
Hebrews 1:3

He came to demonstrate that I am for you,
not against you.
Romans 8:31

And to tell you that I am not counting your sins.
2 Corinthians 5:18-19

Jesus died so that you and I could be reconciled.
2 Corinthians 5:18-19

His death was the ultimate expression
of my love for you.
1 John 4:10

I gave up everything I loved
that I might gain your love.
Romans 8:31-32

If you receive the gift of my son Jesus,
you receive me.
1 John 2:23

And nothing will ever separate you
from my love again.
Romans 8:38-39

Come home and I'll throw the biggest party
heaven has ever seen.
Luke 15:7

I have always been Father,
and will always be Father.
Ephesians 3:14-15

My question is…
Will you be my child?
John 1:12-13

I am waiting for you.
Luke 15:11-32

Love, Your Dad
Almighty God

This compilation of Scriptures captures the loving, caring heart of God toward us. God loves us and says we will have power in this world, and we will do greater things than He did. Well, let's get on to learning what this power is and where it is found.

Chapter 2

GOD CREATED THE UNIVERSE AND HE CREATED YOU

Psalm 19:1

The heavens declare the glory of God; the skies proclaim the work of His hands.

What do you think of when you think of heaven? Do you think of a great big gate with angels standing guard at the entrance? Do you imagine Peter, the disciple, waiting inside the gate and asking, "Why should I let you in?" Do you envision a place of billowy clouds, high in the sky? Have you ever even considered heaven? If not, you must have searched the night skies for the moon or the constellations, or watched the glory of the setting sun? I have always thought that heaven is the place that I will go to when I die. I will live with God, and it is supposed to be a happy place where I will meet up with those who have gone there before me. As a nurse, I have listened to patients who would talk of deceased family members who had come to visit them just a few days before their death. Heaven is the place that most people think of when someone they love has left this world, even if they had never really considered it before. Heaven becomes a very real hope in times of loss. There is a verse in the Bible where Paul says he was caught up to the third heaven, and in Philippians he says that it is better to be away from the body and be in heaven.

I once heard a story about someone who went to heaven and was welcomed by an angel who gave the new arrival a tour. During the tour, they came upon a large vault-like structure with locked drawers and cabinets. The person asked the angel what the drawers and doors were for. The angel responded that they were filled with all the wonderful plans, hopes and dreams that had been waiting to be given to the people on earth, but the things within the drawers had never been claimed or asked for. Many people had desires, dreams and aspirations that were never fulfilled in their lives. They had never stepped out in courage and faith to claim the achievements and things that were still within the drawers. This is a powerful allegory, indicating that there is so much that is still unattained here on earth. Imagine so many dreams left unfulfilled, possessions unclaimed, hopes deferred and actions never taken.

God exhorts us to open our mouth wide and he will fill it. (Psalm 81:10) We do not expect greatness from God or even from ourselves. We do not think of a God who longs to be gracious to us and waits for us to act upon our dreams. The Scriptures also say, "You do not have because you do not ask God." (James 4:2) Jim Rohn wrote, "The worst thing one can do is not to try, to be aware of what one wants and not give in to it, to spend years in silent hurt wondering if something could have materialized - never knowing."

God is a giving God, and He said in John 10:10 that Jesus came so that we would have life and have it abundantly. *Abundance* means no lack and also an overflowing supply. It embodies affluence and bountifulness. When I think of abundance, the question I ask is why is there so much lack, toil and trouble for so many people in the world? We see in the story above that God has so much waiting for people but, for some reason, the majority do not seem to be able to access the gifts that await them in heaven and bring them to earth.

This is a very perplexing situation. I have always wondered

why some people become vastly wealthy, but the majority stay stuck, getting by on a limited supply, without any thought of abundance. They are always thinking of having "just enough", the next paycheque or the next bill payment. Is this why you were created—just to survive and not to thrive—just to be blessed and not to become a blessing? It remains baffling, but there is so much more each of us could accomplish if we only believed, had faith, and went the extra mile with determination. In regard to the very poor, God admonishes that to the person who has been given much, much is required. I believe the intention of this exhortation is for all of us to do something, no matter how small, to help the very poor and the weak. God says he will reward those who give to the poor.

Proverbs 19:17

**Whoever is kind to the poor lends to the Lord,
and he will reward them for what they have done.**

I had a very unique experience, years ago, at a weekend retreat entitled, "The Holy Spirit Weekend". It was a great weekend getaway. My husband and I stayed at a campground and had all of our meals prepared for us. Our mornings and evenings were spent learning about the things of the Holy Spirit. As we were praising the Lord, I felt like I was swept up into the Spirit. In the presence of the Spirit, I began to see picture after picture of the plight of women around the world. I saw visions of women kept under the control of their husbands, sons or another male figure in their lives. Windows were painted black, and the women were imprisoned in their own homes and not allowed out, or even allowed to see out. I saw brothels where young girls were sold over and over, and so much suffering from abuse and a lack of love or protection. I saw women who were taken from their families to become slaves, and girls who were married off much too young. During this experience, I felt the most incredible sense of love surrounding me. It was tender and gentle. The only words to describe it were pure and exquisite love. It was the very essence of perfect love. Remember, God is love.

1 John 4:16

And so we know and rely on the love God has for us. God is love.

As I saw each picture before the eye of my mind, soft tears streamed down my face. I was experiencing the deep sadness that came from the broken heart of God. He was sharing with me His grief. As I was deep in reverie about all that I was feeling and seeing, someone tapped me on the shoulder and the visions stopped. Our inhumanity towards one another causes God so much pain; it grieves Him.

Genesis 6:5-6 (NASB)

Then the Lord saw that the wickedness of man was great on the earth, and that every intent of the thoughts of his heart was only evil continually. 6 The Lord was sorry that He had made man on the earth, and He was grieved in His heart.

When the visions ceased, I became aware once more of the present. The teaching was still going on. I felt like I had left a very safe and protected place. Somehow everything seemed garishly bright, loud and harsh. Oh, how I longed to be back in the presence of the Spirit of the Lord, but the visitation had lifted. I wanted to hold on to the sense of God for as long as I could. I was aware that I had been touched in some way, and a remnant of that mighty Spirit of love was still upon me. The presence was so tender and so easily wounded by complaints, judgments or unkind words. It was such a positive force field of LOVE that I could almost feel it recoil from our judgmental and complaining ways. The Spirit of love wants to uplift, bless and care without any negative force being sent its way. The presence lingered for a while but finally waned out of reach. This experience has stayed fresh in my memory for decades now.

When I think of heaven, I think of the mighty heart of the Lord that will permeate the atmosphere and surround us with His great, kind, gentle, all-consuming love. Trust me; if God is perfect love, you will not be disappointed. During my time as a nurse, I met a couple of patients who had near death experiences and had been face to face with the light of the Lord. They felt such a mighty peace that, when it came time to leave this world, they were expectant and without fear. They were truly embraced in the words of the carpenter's son: "I leave you my peace." in John 14:21. In all the years of my faith in God, I thought only of our lives as lived here on earth, and that one day I would die and go to heaven. My understanding of faith considered only this earth, heaven and hades. One day, all of that simple, limited faith changed, when I viewed a picture of the universe beside a picture of the human brain cell. They were virtually identical. It was sometime later that a verse in Hebrews took on greater meaning. I had never thought of God in relation to the immensity of the universe. And Hebrews clearly states that it is God who created the universe.

Hebrews 1:1-2

In the past God spoke to our ancestors through the prophets at many times and in various ways, but in these last days he has spoken to us by his Son, whom he appointed heir of all things, and through whom also he made the universe.

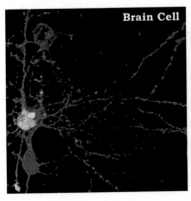

Brain Cell

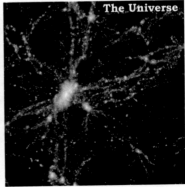

The Universe

The first time I saw this picture of a brain cell, side by side with a picture of the universe, as it went through the news feed on Facebook, I was struck by how much they mirrored each other. They virtually looked like carbon copies of each other. I stopped and wondered how this must be significant and silently asked the Lord what the significance was. I found the mirror images of the brain cell and the universe thought-provoking. Then one day I read:

Ephesians 4:10

He who descended is the very one who ascended higher than all the heavens, in order to fill the whole universe.

My heart leaped when I read these words with the realization that the Spirit of the loving God, whom I knew from the ancient Scriptures, filled the whole universe. I was God-smacked and incredible joy filled me as my heart raced. I thought of the verses that said there was nowhere God was not present. The Psalmist speaks to God declaring:

Psalm 139:7-12

Where can I go from your Spirit?
Where can I flee from your presence?
[8] If I go up to the heavens, you are there;
if I make my bed in the depths, you are there.
[9] If I rise on the wings of the dawn,
if I settle on the far side of the sea,
[10] even there your hand will guide me,
your right hand will hold me fast.
[11] If I say, "Surely the darkness will hide me
and the light become night around me,"
[12] even the darkness will not be dark to you;
the night will shine like the day,
for darkness is as light to you.

Jeremiah 23:23-24
"Am I only a God nearby,"
declares the Lord,
"and not a God far away?
²⁴ *Who can hide in secret places*
so that I cannot see them?"
declares the Lord.
"Do not I fill heaven and earth?"
declares the Lord.

The Spirit of God is omnipresent, which means that He is everywhere. So many people mention the goodness of the universe, and that the universe wants to provide for them. The mention of a personal, loving God seems somewhat difficult for many to accept. After I received that revelation, I could honestly embrace the goodness of the universe, because I know that the loving Spirit of God fills it. Just think of it, the Mighty Spirit of love fills the universe. My thoughts returned to the picture of the universe that was so similar to the human brain cell. My mind went back and forth between the two pictures. I was reminded of the perplexing verse in creation, where God says:

Genesis 1:27

So God created mankind in his own image,
in the image of God he created them;
male and female he created them.

I always wondered about that verse. What part of me was in the image of God? And now before me was a picture where my brain cell was a mirror image of the universe! God said we would have the same power that raised Christ from the dead. Now that was a really big promise to get my head around. I understood where we got our power. It is in our thoughts. Our thoughts are mentioned numerous times in the Bible, so they must be of real significance;

but I wondered how and why. My mind raced at the full realization of all that had been shown to me. God created the universe. God filled the universe. God created you and me in His image. The picture of the brain cell and the image of the universe were the same. God says that:

Proverbs 23:7 (KJV)
For as he thinketh in his heart, so is he:

John 14:12
Very truly I tell you, whoever believes in me will do the works I have been doing, and they will do even greater things than these, because I am going to the Father.

Jesus said we would do greater things than He did. Look at the wonders all around us since the ancient times. My mind was Godsmacked again and I vibrated with pure excitement about the window of wisdom that I was peering into. There was still so much to understand. I thought again about the Almighty God, the Creator of the universe, whose Spirit, filled the Universe. Our brain cells are like tiny sparks of fire seamlessly connected to the Spirit that fills the universe. We have the same DNA of the creative loving Spirit which says, "Whoever believes in me will do even greater works" than Jesus. He has left the same powerful Spirit that raised Christ from the dead within us.... (if we believe). As I considered all of this new information, I concluded again that the power must come from our thoughts.

Wallace D. Wattles states in *The Science of Getting Rich,*

"There is a thinking stuff from which all things are made, and which, in its original state, permeates, penetrates, and fills the interspaces of the Universe. A thought, in this substance, produces the thing that is imaged by the thought. Man can form things in his thought, and, by impressing his thought upon formless substance, can cause the thing he thinks about to be created."

I was struck by the statement about the thinking stuff that fills the interspaces of the universe. It was interesting to find that the interspaces of the universe make up the vast majority of the universe. There are stars, planets and galaxies suspended in the vast space known as dark matter. As I began to compare the universe with the brain, I also found that greater than 90% of the brain is made up of dark matter, which is found between the neurons and ganglia. This was another uncanny similarity, which appeared to be another signpost on my uncharted journey to find the significance of the similarities of the brain and the universe. I needed to understand more.

When you look up into the sky, you see the sun, the moon, the stars, and the galaxies. As I tried to grasp just a bit of the immense, unfathomable reaches of the billions of stars and the billions of galaxies, I was in awe of its beauty, and all the atomic power that is radiated from the sun and from within the stars. Our galaxy is the Milky Way. It has approximately 100-600 billion stars. When we look at the sky, we can only see approximately 2500 of them. The Milky Way Galaxy is 100,000 light years across. Earth is approximately 91 million miles or 149.6 million km from the sun. To look at the pictures sent back by the Hubble Space Telescope is to view ethereal and mysterious beauty, suspended in what appears to be black nothingness. Into this immense infinity of time and space, our teeny, tiny earth is suspended. We live on this teeny, tiny, particle planet called Earth. I agree with King David who wrote:

Psalm 8:1, 3-4

Lord, our Lord,
how majestic is your name in all the earth!
You have set your glory
in the heavens.

³ When I consider your heavens,
the work of your fingers,
the moon and the stars,
which you have set in place,
⁴ what is mankind that you are mindful of them,
human beings that you care for them?

The fact of the matter is, God does care. His love for us is made even clearer in the following two verses:

Deuteronomy 7:6

For you are a people holy to the LORD your God.
The LORD your God has chosen you out of all the peoples
on the face of the earth to be his people, his treasured
possession.

Acts 17:28

'For in him we live and move and have our being.' As some
of your own poets have said, 'We are his offspring.'

I had never noticed the last part of this verse. We are His offspring, His children, with the same likeness and the same powerful spirit of God within us. God wants us to call Him Abba, which is an Aramaic word that expresses warm affection, and actually is translated as *Daddy* or *Father*. Remember Jesus said "Whoever believes in me will have the power to do greater things." The clarification of who He is can be found in the book of John.

John 1:14, 12-13

The Word became flesh and made his dwelling among us.
We have seen his glory, the glory of the one and only Son,
who came from the Father, full of grace and truth. …. ¹² Yet
to all who did receive him, to those who believed in his name,

he gave the right to become children of God—[13] children born not of natural descent, nor of human decision or a husband's will, but born of God.

So, you see, there are a couple of steps necessary in order to become children of God. There is the step of believing and then the step of receiving the Spirit of God. Then we are enabled to discern the things of the Spirit. This is a spiritual birth. It happens when we sincerely ask God to forgive us of all of our wrongdoing, and accept Jesus or Yeshua as Lord and Saviour. There is a Bible story of a boy who suffered from convulsions. The boy's father has trouble believing that Jesus can cure his son. He asks Jesus if He can help his son. Jesus seems perplexed at the question asking Him if He can, and repeats it with an explanation.

Mark 9:20-24

So they brought him. When the spirit saw Jesus, it immediately threw the boy into a convulsion. He fell to the ground and rolled around, foaming at the mouth.
[21] Jesus asked the boy's father,
"How long has he been like this?"
"From childhood," he answered.
[22] "It has often thrown him into fire or water to kill him. But if you can do anything, take pity on us and help us."
[23] "'If you can'?" said Jesus.
"Everything is possible for one who believes."
[24] Immediately the boy's father exclaimed,
"I do believe; help me overcome my unbelief!"

I repeat, "Everything is possible for one who believes." God is a loving God. He loves you, and understands that it is hard to give up our rational way of thinking and live in unfailing faith. God figuratively says, "Believe it and I will prove it to you," but in our limited earthly thinking we say, "Prove it to me and I will believe it." We are a part of God as His offspring, and therefore we are imbued with power. This power is so much greater than our limited earthly bound way of thinking. I felt this power was from our thoughts that flowed from our brains, which are so like the picture of the universe. So I set out to learn more about the universe. As I was searching, I discovered Nikola Tesla. Albert Einstein was asked who he thought was the smartest man in the world. His answer was, "I don't know; you will have to ask Nikola Tesla." Wikipedia states that "Nikola Tesla was a Serbian American inventor, electrical engineer, mechanical engineer, physicist, and futurist best known for his contributions to the design of the modern alternating current (AC) electricity supply system." This brilliant physicist states, "If you wish to understand the universe, think of energy, frequency, and vibration."

The universe is an immense power plant of energy. All of our energy on earth comes from the universe. The sun and the billions upon billions of stars are putting out energy. The sun and the moon produce electro-magnetic radiation, which is converted into energy. This energy can be captured as solar energy which is converted to electricity. If you have a Tesla electric car and you plug it into an outlet of a building powered by solar panels, the Tesla literally runs on the power of the sun. Plants convert the energy of the sun into earthly energy by photosynthesis. We eat the plants and convert the plant energy into fuel for our bodies.

We are composed of intensely vibrating atoms. Everything we are and see is vibrating at incredible speed. The energy produced in every cell of our bodies produces 1000 times more potential energy than that of any atomic bomb used or tested until now. The vibration of these atoms resonates at certain frequencies. When a steel rod is vibrated, the atoms that make up its form create heat. As the speed of vibration increases in intensity, the steel rod will feel warm and then begin to form light as ultraviolet light. This UV light is unseen but will then be transformed to red hot heat which is visible. This red visible heat represents a much higher speed of vibration and energy within the atoms that form the steel rod. It is said that, beyond this intense power of emitted heat and light, we find the powerful vibration level of human *thought*. Thoughts are powerful sources of wave energy which affect the field of energy that surrounds us. The electro-magnetic energy of our thoughts moves up and down in frequencies and vibration. We can have high or low vibrations.

The universe keeps everything in rapid vibration and that creates tremendous power. We are electrically charged beings. Our brain activity is measured with an EEG. Our heart is measured with an ECG. The heart is ten times as strong in electrical energy as the brain. Electricity is the language of communication. Because the energy of the universe is electromagnetic in nature, the atoms of our brains are constantly sending out electro-magnetically charged, wireless thought waves. These thoughts are much like the wireless waves of the wifi network. Our brain is a giant telegraph switching station. Thoughts are almost like a battery, sending charged waves from the body and able to interpret the entangled mass of energy that we perceive as a chair or a coffee pot. Some say we live in a hologram world and that the brain has the ability to interpret it into form. This is getting into amazing quantum physics material, which is far beyond the scope of this book.

Nikola Tesla stated, "My brain is only a receiver, in the Universe there is a core from which we obtain knowledge, strength, and inspiration. I have not penetrated into the secrets of this core but I know that it exists." Alexander Graham Bell said something similar: "What this power is I cannot say; all I know is that it exists and it becomes available only when a man is in that state of mind in which he knows exactly what he wants and is fully determined not to quit until he finds it."

Nikola Tesla did a test on the vibration of sand by applying higher and higher frequencies of sound, which caused the sand to vibrate. You would think that sand bouncing on a metal plate would do just that; bounce around randomly. Well, it does not do that; it forms distinct patterns in resonance with the level of the frequencies. I thought that was enough of a WOW but the fascinating BIG WOW was that, the higher the frequency, the more complex and intricate the patterns became. Sand, in resonance with higher and higher frequencies of vibrating sounds, creates increasingly complex, intricate patterns. This definitely seems to indicate that higher vibrations have more creative energy or power. We are a part of the universe, so this same essence applies to us. We are pure energy; therefore we are emitting energy frequencies and vibrations. This is very interesting and it can be found on YouTube by searching "Amazing Resonance Experiment!" Do not listen to Amazing Resonance 2 since it is deafening and may damage your ears.

James Earl Ray from *The Secret* stated,

"If you were to ask a Quantum Physicist how the universe was made, he would say with energy. Then ask him to describe energy, and he would answer, energy cannot be created or destroyed, always was, always has been. Everything that has ever existed is moving into form, through form and out of form. Ask a theologian what created the universe and he will say God. Ask the theologian to describe God. He would answer God always was, always has been, can never be created or destroyed. God is all that ever was and ever will be, always moving into form, through form and out of form."

Exodus 3:14

God said to Moses, "I am who I am. This is what you are to say to the Israelites: 'I am has sent me to you.'"

"I Am" seems to imply an existence that is not measured by time; it just is, has been, and will continue to be. We are spiritual beings. We live on a small speck of an energy field called Earth, which is operating in a much larger energy field called the universe. Scripture states the universe was created by God, filled by the Spirit of God, and we are made in the image and likeness of God. We are eternal and God has given us the potential to create our own world. Every thought is a wave of energy sent out to the universe we live in. Nikola Tesla stated, "The gift of mental power comes from God, Divine Being, and if we concentrate our minds on that truth, we become in tune with this great power." The question remains: How do we access this power?

Albert Einstein said, "Everything is energy and that is all there is to it. Match the frequency of the reality you want and you cannot help but get that reality. It can be no other way. This is not philosophy. This is physics."

I have already mentioned that I understood from my knowledge of Scripture that the power that God says we have, is within our thoughts. Thoughts are waves of energy. Let's move on to explore more information on our thoughts!

Chapter 3

THE POWER OF YOUR THOUGHTS AND HAVING A VISION

Proverbs 23:7 (KJV)
For as he thinketh in his heart, so is he.

Proverbs 29:18 (KJV)
Where there is no vision, the people perish.

What really is a thought? I found an interesting statement on the internet, in a MIT Engineering article by Elizabeth Dougherty, entitled *What are Thoughts?* She states: "They're really just electro-chemical reactions—but the number and complexity of these reactions make them hard to fully understand." We all have thoughts and electro-chemical power is contained in our thoughts. The Bible has much to say about thoughts. Henry Ford alluded to the level of achievement available within our thoughts in his statement: "Whether you think you can, or think you can't, you are right." Albert Einstein also commented on the power of our thoughts when he said: "The world as we have created it is a process of our thinking. It cannot be changed without changing our thinking." These very successful men acknowledge that there is a starting point to all achievement, and it is in our thoughts. Their statements, just like the Scriptures, state that we become what we think about.

Nothing in our lives happens or changes until the seed of thought is sown. Sometimes our thoughts are spontaneous and we act impulsively and decide quickly. At other times, we mull over our thoughts, slowly forming an image in our mind. Remember, thoughts are vibrations. They are waves of energy, and the thoughts we hold in our mind will gather more power by attracting more energy of the same vibration thus raising us to a higher frequency level. In other words, the thoughts we continually think, become stronger due to the power of Perpetual Transmutation of Energy. The power of energy transmutation is the action of changing a tangible or intangible substance into another form. It is known as the Law of Perpetual Transmutation of Energy. The energy of the universe is constantly moving into and out of form, and the energy of our thoughts has the ability to affect this universal energy that surrounds us.

Proverbs 18:21

The tongue has the power of life and death.

Proverbs 18:21 states the words we speak have the power of life and death. You must realize that not one word is spoken that is not formed first within your mind as a thought. Thoughts precede any word or action taken. Thoughts left unattended have the propensity to be negative. Negative thoughts are self-defeating and very destructive to self esteem, to personal endeavour and achievement. John Assarof states, in his online seminar, *Brainathon*, that the brain is set to anxiety and scarcity. We have to work at it to overcome that negative default mechanism of the brain. Scripture admonishes us to keep our thoughts positive and admonishes us to bring *every* thought captive to the power of positive abundant thinking which empowers us.

2 Corinthians 10:5

⁵ We are destroying speculations and every lofty thing raised up against the knowledge of God, and we are taking every thought captive to the obedience of Christ

Thoughts of fear and worry kill more dreams and hopes than any other emotion. The Bible tells us 365 times "do not fear." It is such an important exhortation that it is repeated enough times to be acknowledged daily. Fear causes confusion and paralysis of action. It is the forerunner that prevents you from reaching all that is your birthright in actualizing your spiritual gifts. Fear puts up blocks in your mind, which prevents you from taking the authentic steps to reach the dream that is within you. Fear keeps you from being your true self or even hearing the whisper of the Spirit, which longs for you to break forth into success! It is said that what you desire to achieve may actually have been planted within your mind by the very God who wants you to attain it.

Thoughts are waves of electro-magnetic energy. They can be positive or negative in nature. Powerful high vibrations of thought and feelings are listed in Galatians as the fruit of the Spirit:

Galatians 5:22-23

But the fruit of the Spirit is love, joy, peace, forbearance [patience], kindness, goodness, faithfulness, ²³ gentleness and self-control.

Thoughts held in these positive emotions are empowering and freeing. We feel whole, centred and happy when we are not troubled or defeated by negative feelings. There is no freedom in fear or a lack of self-confidence, but only a pervasive sense of inadequacy to take action. Fear and negative emotions are of a low vibration. Clinging to them will just strengthen their grip, keeping you defeated. Eliminating fear and negativity is paramount if you want to reach the higher vibrations of love, joy, peace, happiness and greater personal achievement. Persistent anxiety will always be limiting to your success. God is always willing to help us. He is waiting to help, but you still have to do your part. He even says in Jeremiah:

Jeremiah 29:11

For I know the plans I have for you," declares the Lord, "plans to prosper you and not to harm you, plans to give you hope and a future.

God has plans for each of us, but doubt and continual uncertainty of thought will sabotage every endeavour. This is powerfully revealed in the following verses of the ancient scripture:

James 1:5-8

If any of you lacks wisdom, you should ask God, who gives generously to all without finding fault, and it will be given to you.⁶ But when you ask, you must believe and not doubt, because the one who doubts is like a wave of the sea, blown and tossed by the wind.
⁷ That person should not expect to receive anything from the Lord. ⁸ Such a person is double-minded and unstable in all they do.

We cannot achieve anything when we continually waver back and forth in indecision. God cannot bless us either since He says that being double-minded is an unstable mindset. This is not from God because the book of Timothy states:

2 Timothy 1:7

For the Spirit God gave us does not make us timid, but gives us power, love and self-discipline.

God wants you to know that His Spirit will empower you, if you love what you are going after and you go for it with self-discipline. Drifting is not from God; self-discipline is! We all experience fear, but success only comes by taking action. So feel the fear and do it anyway! God may have great plans for you and you may have your own plans, but if you are stuck in fear and negative feelings, achievement of your goals or dreams will remain out of reach. Those plans will remain unfulfilled like the earlier allegory of all the dreams left in the drawers in heaven. Someone said, "Don't ask God to order your steps if you are not willing to move your feet!"

The beginning of mastering fear is when we turn fear into faith in God, whose mighty Spirit of *LOVE* fills the universe. Remember, we are His offspring and like any parent, God's greatest joy is to see you succeed and prosper. He understands you and repeats it over and over again, "Do not fear!" Scripture states:

Isaiah 41:10

So do not fear, for I am with you;
do not be dismayed, for I am your God.
I will strengthen you and help you;
I will uphold you with my righteous
right hand.

There are actors, public speakers, salesmen or entrepreneurs who feel intense fear in their jobs. There are some actors who vomit prior to each performance, but it does not paralyse them from going on stage. They defeat the thoughts of fear by the very act of performing or being present in the moment. They break through the terror barrier and soon realize that the very thing they feared dissolved simply by taking action. It may take repetition to master the intensity of the fear in order to experience the exhilaration of success. Fear is not from God, for God has given us the Spirit of power and that power is released on the highest creative vibration of love. God is the Spirit and that Spirit is *LOVE*. The ancient Scripture says:

1 John 4:18

...perfect love drives out fear...

If your dream is your passion and something you want with all your heart, it will be difficult to get derailed from achieving your desire. Put your heart and soul into your dreams without wavering and apply locked-in, focused action, and you will achieve your desired goal. No barrier, no circumstance, and certainly no fear is going to stop you from achieving your dream. Laser focused thoughts act much like a magnifying glass which can bring beams of sunlight together to burn paper. Without that concentrated beam of power from the sun, the paper remains unchanged. The same thing happens when your thoughts are focused and cannot be deterred. The intensity of your thoughts will cause the Law of Perpetual Transmutation of Energy to change things in your life!

Let us return to the fact that thoughts are waves of energy. The energy released by the heart is ten times greater in electro-magnetic energy than that of the brain, where thoughts originate. When we think of feelings, we think of the heart as the seat of our emotions and the brain as the seat of our thoughts. I had always wondered why God had said,

Proverbs 23:7 (KJV)

For as he thinketh in his heart, so is he.

I repeat this: "For as he thinketh in his *heart,* so is he." Why has God mentioned the thought that takes place within the heart? The revelation came to me when I realized the heart is much more powerful in electro-**MAGNETIC** energy. If you think with your heart, you feel the emotions of excitement, joy, expectation and hope. Emotionalized, heartfelt thought has a much higher vibration, so it is intensely more powerful in attracting and changing the energy field around us. Emotionalized thought actually changes the structure of atoms and energy around us, which attracts what we are earnestly thinking about. It actually raises our vibration to be in resonance with the higher frequency of what we desire.

Remember what Wallace D. Wattles said in *The Science of Getting Rich*?

"There is a thinking stuff from which all things are made, and which, in its original state, permeates, penetrates, and fills the interspaces of the universe. A thought, in this substance, produces the thing that is imaged by the thought. Man can form things in his thought, and by impressing his thought upon formless substance, can cause the thing he thinks about to be created."

Do you see that a thought held in this substance and impressed upon it brings the very things into being? Scripture states that as we sow, so shall we reap. What thoughts are you sowing? Are you focused on empowering thoughts or defeating thoughts?" I always heard T. Harv Ecker say in his trainings, "What you focus on expands." Are you beginning to grasp the immense creative power of your emotionalized, unwavering, focused thoughts? I hope you can understand that God is not the author of negativity, weakness or the dragon of double mindedness. The Bible speaks of an enemy of our souls who would love to keep us drifting in a sea of uncertainty and inactivity with little or no achievement.

Steven Pressfield writes in his book, *The War of Art*:

"Most of us have two lives. The life we live and the unlived life within us. Between the two stands Resistance…Resistance is the most toxic force on the planet. It is the root of more unhappiness than poverty, disease and erectile dysfunction. To yield to Resistance deforms our Spirit. It stunts us and makes us less than we are and were born to be. If you believe in God (and I do) you must declare Resistance evil, for it prevents us from achieving the life God intended when he endowed each of us with our own unique genius…

"Every sun casts a shadow, and genius's shadow is Resistance. As powerful as our soul's call to realization, so potent are the forces of Resistance arrayed against it…Resistance defeats us. Look in your own heart. Unless I am crazy, right now a still small voice is piping up, telling you as it has ten thousand times, the calling that is yours and yours alone. You know it. No one has to tell you. And unless I am crazy, you're not closer to taking action on it than you were yesterday or will be tomorrow. You think Resistance isn't real? Resistance will bury you!"

John Assarof mentions, in his program, *Brainathon*: "The brain has a propensity to think negatively." We are in a daily battle to bring every thought into captivity, into the realm of the power of God. We are in a battle to monitor and capture each thought to stay strong, focused and positive. T. Harv Ecker tells every negative thought "thanks for sharing" and then ignores it. John Assarof also advises, when a negative defeating thought threatens your resolve, you can counteract it by writing down three to five positive thoughts to overcome it.

We are very much a part of the universe and the universal creative force which manifests into form and function. What we perceive as solid substance is a mass of vibrating atoms. Everything is alive with subatomic, electro-magnetic power. Thoughts are powerful force fields. They can be positive and empowering, thus vibrating on higher frequencies. Higher frequencies attract more of what is good and desirable to our lives. Our thoughts can also be negative and self-defeating. These are of a very low frequency. Low frequency, negative thoughts attract more of what we do not want and actually repel what we do want.

Please remember, there is an adversarial force that is contrary to the will of God, and it will do everything in its power to keep you from achieving success. It will do this because, "being profoundly effective is glorifying to God," as I have heard Beth Moore state in a Bible study I attended. So stay positive and do not complain about circumstances. "When you complain, you are a giant crap magnet!" is something that I have heard T. Harv Ecker exclaim in his seminars.

When we think of something that we love and we hold onto that thought, it will attract other energy in resonance with its vibration. This power of thought increases until the thought becomes an idea. This idea may become something that we become fascinated with and fixated upon. Then the idea takes hold of us and may grow into the very purpose of our life. Have you ever felt like you have floundered in failure, searching for the purpose that is searching for you? Have you tried and tried, over and over, forever searching and never finding? Even if you have that great job or career, there is something haunting the recesses of your mind, searching for more. I believe that there is something that is to be fulfilled by each one of us, but often it remains elusive.

Sometimes I wonder if the increase in illness, depression and suicide is because our lives are filled with the ever-present empty noise of TV, the Internet and cell phones. I think many of us drift through life, going to work, and silencing the thought that longs to be heard. There was a time when I filled my days with just aimless use of the computer and then planned my evenings around what I was going to watch on TV. Each day was spent without worth or achievement. I used to wonder if this was all there was to live out my days. The void felt like a massive empty cavern in my life. Do you find that TV, computers and cell phones ubiquitously fill every empty space of time in your life?

I was out for dinner recently and a young couple was sitting across from each other. Both of them had their heads down in their cell phones. There did not seem to be any connection to one another. I come from a generation that did not always have our ears filled with ear buds connected to some device to walk to work, go for a run, sit in a restaurant or wait in a line. I wonder, if God took the time to speak to us, could we hear Him?

I have heard the voice of God once. It was an external audible voice. I was walking through my living room and distinctly heard a voice say to me, "Richard is going to die before you." I was shocked and disturbed, and mentioned it to my daughter as I turned into the kitchen. Her response was, "Mom, don't say that!" God also speaks to us through the word of the Scriptures. I remember reading my Bible at our cottage, as Richard worked outside. It was from the book of Isaiah.

Isaiah 41:13

For I am the LORD your God who takes hold of your right hand and says to you, Do not fear; I will help you.

The words leaped off the page and I stopped and asked God, "Why are you going to hold my hand?" Just days later, my husband Richard suffered a cardiac arrest, was admitted to hospital and, five days later, passed away. Not only did God hold my hand through the love of so many people, but he had also, in some way, prepared me for what was to come. Through the whole experience, our family was upheld in supernatural grace in our time of grief. I often wonder what frequency I was on that I was able to tune into the voice of God as I casually walked through my living room.

God speaks in whispers and, even if He did speak, would we be in resonance with the frequency of His voice? We find this mentioned in 1 Kings. God spoke in a whisper to the frightened and defeated prophet Elijah.

1 Kings 19:11-13

The Lord said, "Go out and stand on the mountain in the presence of the Lord, for the Lord is about to pass by." Then a great and powerful wind tore the mountains apart and shattered the rocks before the Lord, but the Lord was not in the wind. After the wind there was an earthquake, but the

Lord was not in the earthquake.[12] After the earthquake came
a fire, but the Lord was not in the fire. And after the fire
came a gentle whisper. [13] When Elijah heard it,
he pulled his cloak over his face and went out and stood
at the mouth of the cave.

Then a voice said to him, "What are you doing here, Elijah?"

I read somewhere that only those who are on the same frequency can truly hear us. So if people do not listen to us, it is not a personal rejection, but reveals they are not in resonance with our message. They are tuned to a totally different frequency. God speaks in whispers and His frequency is love. When we love, we are dialled into God. God is ready to bless abundantly.

1 Corinthians 2:9

However, as it is written:
"What no eye has seen,
what no ear has heard,
and what no human mind has conceived"
the things God has prepared for those who love him

Ephesians 2:10

For we are God's handiwork, created in Christ Jesus to do
good works, which God prepared in advance for us to do.

Do you see how there is something in this verse that suggests we have been created to achieve something that is unique to each one of us? Amazingly, it might actually be imprinted in our very DNA. The above verse states there is something good each of us is to achieve.

I searched forever for my purpose and could not find what it was. Yes, I was a nurse and happy to be one, but there was something seeking me and I could not grasp what it was. I was always searching for something. I perceived it would be in a network marketing business. I tried so many business ventures, and in all of them I would have clarity one day and then lose the vision shortly after. No vision ever stuck. I was in dismay since all the plans I would make and the steps I was going to take always dissipated into nothingness. I am sure all my dreams failed because they were not the path I was meant to be on. Something within me always called me back to the search for that call upon me which I did not know. I am now retired and, in the last couple of years, something has gripped me and become my holy obsession. It is my vision that brings me great satisfaction, and it is something that settles and defines me.

Proverbs 29:18 (KJV)
Where there is no vision, the people perish:

It is my vision to post Scripture on Facebook. It was my hope that my daily posts would go far and wide around the world. I began posting Scripture and praise to counteract all the darkness of ISIS which was coming through the news feed of Facebook. It was my daily passion to search the Scriptures first thing in the morning, in order to select the verses to post. I would always ask for guidance from above. I was frightened, since there seems to be an anti-Christian sentiment in our society. Day after day I would post to nobody and nothing. It was a lonely slog when I would see so many likes and comments on other posts. I felt so alone, but every day I would wake with anticipation to send another pearl of wisdom from the Word of God into the world.

I posted publicly, hoping to reach as many people as possible. Every day I prayed over the post and asked God to touch the lives of those who could benefit from the encouragement of His Word. I longed for the likes and the shares to send the post further and further into the world. The Bible verses remained like silent sentinels on my wall. Day after day, feeling insignificant and invisible, I posted. I wanted to stop but some force held me to my task.

My solitary activity continued until, one day, I said to the

Lord, "I am going to stop if there is not one *like* on the post." The next morning I checked, and there were three! I was encouraged to continue. Sometimes I would put up my post, and then felt like I wanted to run and hide. At other times, I would close the computer and not open it till the next day. Eventually the ritual of being faithful to the daily activity gave me the ability to accept that the Word of God appeared to be relevant to only a few.

I faced the fear of what appeared to be my meaningless daily activity without fail. As time went on, a few faithful souls began to stand by me. They meant more to me than they will ever know. They kept me going. Every day, I held the vision before me of God's Word outstretched like loving arms encircling the globe. I felt my impact was so small. There was no greater passion than my Lord and sharing His Word, but I felt the force that had compelled me lift after 450 consecutive days.

When I stopped my Facebook posts, the same thought that always lurked in the recesses of my mind pursued me with even greater strength. What was my purpose? Then I saw the quote by Bishop T.D. Jakes, which stated,

"If you can't figure out your purpose, figure out your passion.
For your passion will lead you right into your purpose."

I remember the day that I saw this quote, my mind scrolled through all the business ventures that I had tried and failed at, even while I was a nurse. I could not understand what was calling to me. Then a gentle thought passed through my mind. I looked helplessly to the ceiling and said to the Lord, "Well, I suppose, Lord, You are my passion. That is great, Lord, You are my passion, but how do I monetize that?" I needed to generate an income. I cannot charge for a Bible study or prayer. I just figured that there was no way to pursue God as my passion. I was not a theologian or a pastor, so I dropped the thought. But I knew God had heard the cry of my heart. It was shortly afterwards that I felt led to stop my daily posting. It was like being released from a calling.

Now my passion was clear, but could it really be my purpose? I mulled it over and was led to take the review for a course that I had previously taken with Raymond Aaron on writing a book. My passion was morphing into another form. As I thought more and more about writing this book, I realized that I felt spiritually weaker without my posts. Shortly afterwards, I resumed my daily Facebook posts, which strengthened me greatly in the Spirit. I continue to post Scripture daily. You can follow me on Facebook, under Jennifer Kiyonaga, if you are interested.

My vision still compels me to reach out and touch the world with the love of God. I know this is my ultimate life purpose. Though I do not know how I am to achieve this, I do know each step will be revealed, as I step forward in faith. Each day my vision attracts more ideas and paths to take, to fully actualize all that is being unveiled in my heart. God has called me to share *His* love with you. I know that you are dear to Him. Remember, the Lord *treasures* you. Though my path before me is unknown, I trust the Lord will order my steps. One of the first verses I memorized is below:

Proverbs 3:5-6

*Trust in the Lord with all your heart
and lean not on your own understanding;
in all your ways submit to him,
and he will make your paths straight.*

Jesus was a man of action. He admonished His followers to "Go the extra mile." So, whatever it is you want to achieve, you need to feel it with anticipation, as if you were thinking with your heart and do more than is expected of you.

Review your dreams, let your imagination add more details to get you excited for your purpose, and go that extra mile to achieve it. Get creative in achieving what you want. What is your vision? Do you have a clear picture in your mind about what you wish to achieve? Do you have something you desire in your heart, but think it is impossible? Is your dream something that is just a defeated thought held captive by self-doubt and indecisiveness? Fear can be mastered, and the choice is yours as to how you handle it. The Bible says:

Joshua 24:15

But if serving the Lord seems undesirable to you, then choose for yourselves this day whom you will serve.

Do you choose to focus on fear and empower it, or do you want to defeat it by rising above it and breaking through it? You have a choice, as seen below. Which interpretation do you choose? Alex Guillen, the very successful Marketing Guy, shared these statements regarding fear at an *Empowering Women to Succeed* event:

Fear---False Evidence Appearing Real
Fear---Fear Everything and Run
Fear--- Face Everything and Rise

The Scriptures say 365 times "Do not fear."

God's benevolent power is available to you. God longs to help, strengthen and bless you. Expand your thought for that car, home, mission trip, or the new business by adding the details. Turn the thought into a vision. See it! What does it look like? What is the colour? Who is with you in the vision? How do you feel? Remember, the Lord says:

Proverbs 23:7 (KJV)

For as he thinketh in his heart, so is he.

You have to feel the emotions in your thought, the happiness, the fulfillment of your dreams, and it may become your very purpose!

Have you ever heard of anyone telling you to think with your heart? We say we have a happy heart or a broken heart. We feel from our heart, and it is out of the heart that a man speaks, says the Lord. The power of our thoughts is magnified when all the aspects of a vision are seen and experienced with feeling. Some people have trouble seeing their vision in their mind. Seeing your vision in your mind is imperative to achieving it. Imagination is the wonderful faculty that carries us far and wide. Imagination sets us free, but often what we see we perceive as impossible. Everything that you perceive as impossible contains the word possible! Scripture says:

Philippians 4:13 (NKJV)
I can do all things through Christ who strengthens me.

Did that statement say "a few things"? No, it said I can do ALL things through Christ, who is also the one through whom God says He created the universe! Bob Proctor likes to say that the biggest challenge to achievement is having "a poverty of imagination and a weakness of focus!" When we lose focus, we give up, and the drifting thoughts become the wandering focus where nothing can ever be achieved. Drifting is like the waves tossed back and forth going nowhere. Raymond Aaron likes to say, "Most people live in a sea of sameness and never climb aboard the Island of Individuality!" So go for your dream!

Rob Giltanen said: "Here's to the crazy ones. The misfits. The rebels. The troublemakers. The round pegs in the square holes. The ones who see things differently. They're not fond of rules. And they have no respect for the status quo. You can quote them, disagree with them, glorify or vilify them. About the only thing you can't do is ignore them. Because they change things. They push the human race forward. And while some may see them as the crazy ones, we see genius. Because the people, who are crazy enough to think they can change the world, are the ones who do."

Wise Maya Angelou is quoted as saying, "A single fantasy can change a million realities."

Think of those visionaries that have impacted millions of

realities. They had a vision, a dream, or a picture of something that they wanted to achieve, without ever giving up on it. All of these visionaries started with a thought that became an idea which grew into a VISION. They did not have a roadmap, but they had unwavering faith and dedicated determination to achieve what they could see. The deed was complete once the DECISION was made to achieve it. Here is a very short list of a few of them.

Henry Ford—the Model T

Thomas Edison—the light bulb, among many other things

The Wright Brothers—the airplane

Banting and Best—insulin

Bill Gates—Windows software

Steve Jobs—Apple- He said, "The vision will possess you and you will not need be pushed"

Oprah Winfrey—TV show, print magazine, her OWN TV station, and so much philanthropy

Alexander Graham Bell—the telephone

The list is endless of those who had nothing but a dream, an idea, or a vision. They held their vision with passion and heartfelt determination to achieve it. There was no obstacle that could defeat the dream that possessed them. They almost all agree that there is an unknown Power that exists. God said, "I AM," which implies a source of power without beginning or end, and available to all.

What is your dream? Are you leaving it unfulfilled in your drawer in heaven? Are you going to make it happen or are you going to leave it there? What is it that you want, that you desire with all your heart, energy and mind? Send your vision out to the universal Spirit of God. It will come to be, if you hold it fast with faith. Your vision can be strengthened by creating a vision board.

Place pictures of the things that you desire onto a board. This will help your mind see what your heart desires every day! Look at your pictures, think about them, and feel how great it is going to be to possess or achieve what they represent. Bob Proctor carries a vision card in his pocket at all times, and he feels the vision within and reads the card frequently. The desire is cherished, reviewed and given heartfelt attention to create the vibration that will bring it to being. You are in the process of retraining your subconscious to embrace the new reality you desire. The creation of your vision board strengthens your vision. Raising your vibration is important to be in resonance with the higher level of frequency of your vision or dream.

I raise my vibration by prayer, meditation, playing praise music loudly or through head phones. The praise plays out at times in my mind always returning me to a sense of trust and peace. I sit quietly with a candle and read my Bible. I have overcome so many obstacles in my life that I now just think of a challenging event with. "This too shall pass." I have included a list from Sandy Gallagher on fifteen ways to raise your vibration plus six ways to take better care of your body which Scripture calls the Temple of the Holy Spirit.

15 Ways to Raise Your Vibration, by Sandy Gallagher of the Proctor Gallagher Institute.

"Our inner world creates the outer world. In other words, our vibration, or the pattern of our thoughts, attitudes, and actions, is what creates our reality. That's because, unlike what past scientific theories assumed, the space around us is not empty. It is full of a living essence, which is like a conduit that carries our mental frequencies out into the field of possibility.

Another false assumption from the past is that our external circumstances just happen. They don't. We create them. Like oscillations of a bowed string, the notes we play do matter. So, if you want to change what you experience, then you must change your vibration. There are countless ways to do this, but here are a few that work for me:

Stimulate Your Mind

1. **Become conscious of your thoughts.** Everything you think, say, or feel becomes your reality. So pay attention to what's going on in your mind and take steps to turn things around when appropriate. For example, the next time a negative thought pops into your head, take the time to acknowledge it, ask yourself if the idea is true or if it is beneficial to you, and then dismiss it and turn it around for the positive.

2. **Read a high vibe book.** If you know much about Bob and me, you know how important we think reading personal development books is. I study every day, and I always feel better after reading than I did before.

    Reading high vibration books, like *Think and Grow Rich, You2, Your Invisible Power, The Science of Getting Rich* (and thousands of other books), regularly will not only make you feel better, it will transform your life.

3. **Visualize and meditate.** Too often, we rush through our days with a scattered brain, leaving us in a state of chaos and anxiety. Visualization and meditation not only put you in a peaceful state of mind, but they also help attract what you want in life. Just 10 to 15 minutes a day can do wonders for your vibration.

4. **Find something beautiful and appreciate it.** Beauty is all around us, yet so often we walk around with blinders on. Stop rushing for a moment, and take the time to look around or stand in the sun and appreciate your surroundings.

5. **Repeat affirmations.** Say things that inspire you 100

times a day. They can [be] simple statements like I am happy, I am prosperous, or I am unafraid of change. You may not believe it yet, but with practice, you will.

6. **Set a positive intention before going to bed.** Just before you go to sleep at night, set an intention to enjoy the next day. Imagine wonderful things happening from the time you get up until you go to bed. You'll be amazed at the impact this has on your outlook and experiences.

Change Your Focus

1. **Write down ten things you are grateful for.** This is such a beautiful exercise. Making a gratitude list shifts your vibration from focusing on what you don't have to what is already abundant in your life. And that sends out a message that you want more to be grateful for.

2. **Send love to three people who are bothering you.** I do this after I complete my gratitude list each morning. It may not be easy to do at first but, I promise, it will lift your spirits and make you feel freer every time you do it.

3. **Be kind to others.** Giving to someone else (without expecting anything in return) shifts your thinking from "I don't have enough," or "Woe is me," to "I have more than enough to give to others." Abundance is a high vibration.

4. **Laugh.** There is nothing like a good laugh to improve your mood and raise your energetic state. Osho once said, "Life as such has to be taken as cosmic joke – and then suddenly you relax because there is nothing to

be tense about. And in that very relaxation something starts changing in you."

Lightheartedness is the best way to approach almost all dilemmas in your life. When you are in a fight or an argument with someone, try to administer a little bit of humour to the situation. It can change the whole energy field of the room. If you are in a negative circle of thinking, refer back to something that made you laugh in the past. It's never worth it to not be at peace.

5. **Listen to music you love.** The music shifts your frequency by making you happy.

6. **Say something nice to a stranger.** Your words matter. Using them to uplift others puts you in a high vibration. Your vibration suffers when you gossip or speak poorly of others.

Change Your Environment

1. **Walk in nature.** Our bodies need natural light (sunshine) and natural air. Nature provides harmonic frequencies that are compatible with our personal frequencies. The natural sounds of birds singing and wind moving through the trees help us reduce stress, which, in turn, elevates our vibration frequency.

   If you don't want to walk, find yourself a patch of earth, kick your shoes off to reconnect with Mother Earth. She will work her magic.

2. **De-clutter your space.** A disorganized, untidy, clutter-filled work and living space is both a symptom and a source of stress. Clean up the mess and you'll ramp up your vibration.

3. **Bring in fresh flowers.** Flowers in your home instantly improve your mood, and can help you feel less worried and anxious.

Here in the additional six ways to encourage you to take care of your body, as mentioned by Sandy Gallagher.

Be Aware of Your Body

1. **Be conscious of the foods you eat.** You've heard the saying, "You are what you eat." If you want to raise your vibration, eat foods with high frequencies (such as fruits and vegetables). Start paying attention to how certain foods make your body feel.
2. **Drink water.** Always drink plenty of water to assist your body in flushing out toxicity day to day. Toxicity has a marked impact on our vibration, so we must do what we can to reduce its impact within and around us.
3. **Get your blood pumping.** The more you move, the higher your vibration goes. So get active. Dance, jog, move your body!
4. **Do yoga or a similar practice** that aims to shift your mental vibration.
5. **Jump up and down.** Research shows that the simple action of jumping excites the cells in the body and makes them healthier.
6. **Take a shower or bath** to wash off the stress and elevate your vibration.

The Law of Vibration is real. Your energy frequency and vibration directly relate to both your thoughts and your surroundings. So, if something resonates at a stronger energetic frequency than you do, that level of frequency pulls you in like a whirlpool.

For that reason, be aware of what's going on inside you and around you. Surround yourself with what you want in life, fill your mind with positivity and purpose, send love to all those around you, and live every day with good intentions.

To more and better,
Sandy Gallagher

You can see that it is imperative to stay positive, and remain uplifted and uplifting.

Bob Proctor states in *You Were Born Rich*:

"Even Jesus tried to tell the world as he was doing His great work some two thousand years ago, that you too were capable of doing what he was doing. In fact, He even went a step further in saying, 'even greater things you are capable of.' Believe Him, He spoke the truth. The little people will say, that is not what He meant. But let me assure you, it is exactly what he meant. If you can see it and believe it –you can do it."

Napoleon Hill said in the book *Think and Grow Rich*: "whatever the mind can conceive and believe it can achieve." He also said, "Persistence is the key."

Remember, everything is made of waves of powerful energy which comes from billions of atoms that create everything. We are like human transmission towers. Energy is always changing. We grow older; plants change each day; concrete is aging and developing cracks; trees go through the seasons. Nothing is static. Perpetual Transmutation of Energy is constant. When you think and create images in your mind, and then hold those images, by law they *must* move into form within and through you. We are pure spiritual energy. Bob Proctor states: "Every thought that you think and dwell on is beginning to move into form. The thoughts that you are thinking about are moving into condition, circumstance and results by the Law of Perpetual Transmutation of Energy."

We are part of this vast, immeasurable energy field called the universe and the Spirit of God fills the universe. We are surrounded by Divine Spirit energy. We are seamlessly a part of this force. This great power is accessed through our minds, within our brains, and the communication with this source is two-way. When we send our thoughts, which are really vibration impulses to God, into the universe, we are much like a radio or TV station which is transmitting silent signals, searching for receptive receivers in resonance with the signal. If our thoughts are not crystal clear and steady, it is much like the static of a poor radio signal. If the message of what is truly desired is unclear, the waffling person will have difficulty achieving anything. If the vision is clear, detailed, and sustained with the energy and feeling of the heart, it must come into form by law. Once you have your vision, you must take inspired, consistent action toward achieving your goal of having a successful business, creating art or receiving some other desired outcome.

Steven Pressfield writes in his book, *The War of Art*:

"...the most important thing about art is to work. Nothing else matters except sitting down every day and trying.

Why is this important?

Because when we sit down day after day and keep grinding, something mysterious starts to happen. A process is set into motion by which, inevitably and infallibly, heaven comes to our aid. Unseen forces enlist in our cause; serendipity reinforces our purpose.

....When we sit down day after day and do our work, power concentrates around us. The Muse takes note of our dedication. She approves. We have earned favour in her sight. When we sit down and work, we become like a magnetized rod that attracts iron filings. Ideas come. Insights accrete.

Just as Resistance has its seat in Hell, so Creation has its home in Heaven. And it's not just a witness, but an eager active ally…

We're facing dragons too. Fire breathing griffins of the soul, whom we must outfight and outwit to reach the potential of our self-in-potential and to release the maiden who is God's plan and destiny for ourselves and the answer to why we were put on this planet."

This beautifully written piece of literature truly captures the essence of our "Divine Ally" who waits to come to our assistance and help us reach that which we were created for. It also highlights that Resistance is going to do all it can to defeat us every step of the way. So, realize that we are in a battle to reach our highest potential, and to fully actualize our visions, dreams and goals. Waffling, wavering and procrastination are from Resistance who in the spirit realm is our arch enemy.

There are still other things that we can do to nurture and strengthen the process of empowerment from God.

Chapter 4

THE POWER OF PRAYER

1 Thessalonians 5:16-18

Rejoice always, pray continually, and give thanks in all circumstances; for this is God's will for you in Christ Jesus.

Have you ever prayed? Was it in a time of need? Sadly, it is only in times of need that many people pray. I know life is easy without prayer, because life is very manageable when it is going smoothly. People tend to look to a higher Source of Power for encouragement and strength when illness and tragedy strikes. I used to only pray when I had a need or a great desire for something. It is unfortunate that the Lord is just an afterthought until life slips off the rails. It is when the tough times come that people tune into the things of the Spirit. How sad! Why is it that reliance on God becomes relevant only when circumstances appear beyond our control, or too painful to handle alone in this earthly realm?

When I was a nurse, it was so sad to see people who had no time at all for God in this life, until their life was ending. Many, at this time, were so fearful of the unknown that they were willing to embrace a God whom they had shunned their whole life. And God was faithful as He reached down in compassion to those who were weak and heavy laden, and lifted them up. His Spirit was always loving and gracious. God became such a comfort to those who had never acknowledged Him until they were at the end of their own resources in this world. God longs to be gracious and loving to you. He wants to hear what it is that you desire. He wants to be a part of your life; so take time to tell Him what it is that you want! Make this your prayer, even if it is your very first prayer! Ask in prayer!

Matthew 7:7-8

Ask, Seek, Knock
Ask and it will be given to you; seek and you will find; knock and the door will be opened to you. [8] For everyone who asks receives; the one who seeks finds; and to the one who knocks, the door will be opened.

1 Thessalonians 5:16-18(NASB)

Rejoice always; [17] pray without ceasing;
[18] in everything give thanks; for this is God's will for you in Christ Jesus.

Prayer is coming before the throne of grace. We are to ask in prayer continually. The verse above says, "Pray without ceasing," which seems like a tall order. It almost seems like it would be a challenge to keep that practice up. So, what does it mean to pray without ceasing? It is to go about our day with a God consciousness. It is to know that the Spirit is everywhere; present at all times, and always close at hand. I can honestly say that I talk to God the whole day through! When I wake, my day starts with, "Good Morning, Lord!" and from there it continues. Just today, a friend came over to fix some lights, and asked if I had some duct tape. I knew that I did but, as I searched, I could not find the tape. I then asked the Lord, "Do you know where it is, Lord?" and immediately I reached behind something, and there it was! I am conscious that His Spirit is within me. The Spirit of the Lord knows our thoughts, so why not include God in our daily lives? Remember, He asks us to call Him *Abba* or *Father*. God is omniscient and omnipresent, which means that He is all-knowing and present everywhere at all times. His Spirit fills the whole universe. There is no request that is too small for Him, as some seem to think. God is interested in the details of your life. Scripture says even the hairs on your head are counted. It is said in Matthew:

Matthew 6:26-27

Look at the birds of the air; they do not sow or reap or store away in barns, and yet your heavenly Father feeds them. Are you not much more valuable than they? Can any one of you by worrying add a single hour to your life?

We see here that God is trying again to reassure us that we are very valuable to Him, and that worrying, much like fear, does not accomplish anything. He loves to show Himself strong on our behalf. I have heard many stories from people, especially from missionaries, about how God has divinely intervened to answer their seemingly impossible prayers. There is a verse that says that the faith of a mustard seed can move mountains. That seemed truly impossible until I heard the story about an orphanage in a Far East country. The orphanage was in a valley, overshadowed by a mountain which greatly reduced the sunlight to the village and made growing food difficult. The children knew what the Word of God said about faith and the mountain. They said they would pray to God to move the mountain like He said. The missionary teacher was concerned the children would be disappointed, but the prayers of the children were constant and their childlike faith unwavering! Well, it was not long before the military showed up and needed a port in the nearby harbour. They proceeded to dynamite the mountain for fill and, as the mountain moved into the sea, the sun shone brighter into the village. The children never waivered in their prayers to the faithful God who longs to show Himself strong on behalf of those who come to him in faith.

Jeremiah 32:27

I am the LORD, the God of all mankind.
Is anything too hard for me?

Another prayer that seemed impossible was by a missionary in Africa, who had a very sick patient with a life-threatening fever. The people began to pray and ask God to intervene and give them ice. Then there was a hailstorm, and large balls of ice lay before them in abundance to cool the sick patient! God hears and can provide what is apparently impossible. Remember those visionaries, like Alexander Graham Bell and Thomas Edison, who had nothing but a dream or a picture in their mind. The same applies to so many others around the world who see something in their mind that they are led to achieve.

Huldah and Mark Buntain went to India in 1954. They planned to stay a year. Huldah was very reluctant to go with a new baby. She took comfort in the fact that they only planned to stay for one year. The smells and what she saw upon arrival nauseated her. However, that one year has extended to over 60 years of service and aid to the people of Calcutta. After years of helping the people, they wanted to build a hospital in Calcutta. Calcutta is a very congested city and there was not much land available for building. They prayed for land. They were given an old British cemetery which had never been used. When the foundation was being dug, it filled with water and the site was not considered good for building. Mark Buntain said a prayer of faith on top of the endless prayers that had already been prayed for the hospital. As he stood beside the pit, Mark tied a string around a tiny Bible and lowered it into the water as the faithful of their ministry watched. As they prayed, the water began to recede, and soon there was no water left in the foundation pit. It never returned! Can you imagine the thrill of seeing this full blown miracle happening before their very eyes! Scripture states:

Matthew 19:26

Jesus looked at them and said,
"With man this is impossible, but with God
all things are possible."

Years later the Buntains were given an MRI machine which had to be kept very dry. Huldah Buntain told the installers that it had to go into the basement. It was thought to be a very unsuitable site until the installers drilled holes through the wall to find the ground was bone dry around the foundation of the building. Calcutta is a low lying city—almost at sea level—and is prone to floods, so even this finding seemed extraordinary.

The Buntains had a standing order that no patient of Mother Teresa was ever to be turned away from their hospital, and they were great friends and supporters of her ministry. The Calcutta Mercy Ministries has rescued countless children off the streets of Calcutta. The ministry has educated, housed, and taught them life skills. Many are employed in the very ministry that raised them. They are nurses, doctors, seamstresses and some also hold positions in business. Those who were once lost are now in positions of leadership and are teaching and mentoring new generations of the forsaken in Calcutta. The various diverse outreach ministries reach many who are lost, alone and without hope on the streets or the garbage dumps of Calcutta. The one year ministry that Hulda Buntain was reluctant to experience turned into her life purpose, even after her husband Mark, who was the founder of the Ministry, passed away. It was her friend, Mother Theresa, who encouraged her to continue the work after Mark's death. Sometimes what you resist the most in life is exactly where you will find your purpose.

**Huldah Buntain planned to stay only one year in India,
but has spent over 60 years in Calcutta.**

To learn more of Mark and Huldah Buntain and their incredible achievements in India look up her non-profit site, Calcutta Mercy Ministries at www.calcuttamercy.org

I feel honoured to be allowed to share just a bit about this great ministry of mercy, which has touched thousands of lives in over sixty years of service in India. Huldah and her late husband, Mark, have fulfilled the great calling of faith that the Lord asks of us all. There are so many who have fulfilled this mighty calling throughout the world.

James 1:27

*Religion that God our Father accepts as pure and faultless
is this: to look after orphans and widows in their distress
and to keep oneself from being polluted by the world.*

Personally, I have experienced the provision of God in so many ways. I will share one of my experiences of answered prayer. I had a friend who was leaving Toronto and she really wanted a copy of the NIV Bible that I was using. My husband was on a trainee salary and I was a stay-at-home mother for our two children. Money was tight. I began to pray about how I could give my friend the Bible before she left Toronto. Then, one day, I just decided that I would go and buy the Bible and sacrifice something else. I really believed that God would provide, but I did not know how or when. As I left the house to take my children to a doctor's appointment, I looked up and spoke to the sky, "Lord, I know you will provide."

At the doctor's office, I began chatting with another mother. When I was called into the examining room, she said she would wait for me, so we could continue our conversation. I told her that I wanted to go to the Canadian Bible Society to purchase an NIV Bible for a friend. She was so excited to tell me that somebody had just given her five gift-boxed NIV Bibles. They told her to give them to anyone who wanted one! My happiness was unbounded and my gratitude immense. That day remains one of the most memorable in my journey of faith. I thought my provision would come one day in some other form, like a forgotten cheque owed to me. Can you imagine, as a new Christian, how much this gift meant to me and how it strengthened my trust in God's provision? God has proven, over and over again, that He hears my prayers—even the ones that I have thought of, but never spoken.

Let's take a deeper look at prayer. Is prayer that thing we do on our knees beside our bed? "Good night, God bless, keep me till the morning light." Is it something you read from a prayer book? God says to come boldly before the throne, which is a throne of grace! Can you imagine entering boldly before God, then putting your head down and reading a prayer that someone else wrote and published long ago? I believe that the answer should be no. God already knows what you need or desire but He delights to hear it from you.

When my husband was dying in the hospital, the chaplain came by and I asked him if we could pray together for my husband. He appeared befuddled and lost, and told me that he did not have his prayer book with him, and so he could not pray. I told him I could pray, and so I did, for the both of us. I could not imagine having my prayers of faith reduced to what was printed in some dusty old volume, written in formal precision of thought and word long ago. I feel prayers from a book seem inauthentic, and impersonal. I want God to hear prayers that come from my heart. I truly felt sorry for the chaplain who could not approach the throne of grace in his own words.

So what exactly is prayer? Charles Spurgeon writes in the book, *The Power of Prayer in a Believer's Life,*

"True prayer is an approach of the soul by the Spirit of God, to the throne of God. It is not the utterance of words, it is not alone the feelings of desire, but it is the advance of the desires to God, the spiritual approach of our nature toward the Lord our God. True prayer is neither a mental exercise nor a verbal performance. It is far deeper than that. It is a spiritual transaction with the Creator of heaven and earth. God is Spirit, unseen of mortal eye and only to be perceived by the inner man. Our spirit within us ....discerns the Great Spirit, communes with Him, presents to Him its requests, and receives from Him answers of peace."

How does God feel about us coming to Him in prayer? God has an open door policy! The Bible says to come boldly to the throne of grace. We can come to Him with any request. He knows what is best for us and the answer may be a yes, or a no, or slow in coming.

Hebrews 4:16 (NKJV)
Let us therefore come boldly to the throne of grace,
that we may obtain mercy and find grace to help in
time of need.

Psalm 37:4 (NASB)

Delight yourself in the Lord; And He will give you the desires of your heart.

If God is your delight, then it is easy to figure that your heart will be in alignment with His mighty heart of love. Did you know there is only one mediator between God and man, and that mediator is Jesus? (1 Timothy 2:5)

Romans 8:34

Christ Jesus who died—more than that, who was raised to life—is at the right hand of God and is also interceding for us.

Hebrews 4:15

For we do not have a high priest who is unable to empathize with our weaknesses, but we have one who has been tempted in every way, just as we are—yet he did not sin.

Our high priest is the one who calls you friend, and the one who paid the price to purchase your pardon before a holy, righteous God. There is no greater love than to lay down your life for another. Well, that is exactly what the One who intercedes on our behalf has done.

Hebrews 7:25

Therefore he is able to save completely those who come to God through him, because he always lives to intercede for them.

Jesus wants our best and our success. He wants to assist us in our endeavours. The verses above say that He empathizes with us and now intercedes on our behalf. He understands because He has experienced this life. He often gives birth to a desire within our minds in order to help us achieve the very thing He wants to achieve through us. If we trust Him, even when we do not understand, He promises to direct our paths. The Bible states:

James 4:8 (NKJV)
Draw near to God and He will draw near to you.

Here we see the two-way action of moving toward each other. We have to do some moving toward God and He will come near to us. It is prayer that brings us to God, heartfelt prayer. Turn that idea, that vision, that desire into a prayer and you will spiritually enhance the strength of its vibration.

Psalm 23:7 (KJV)
For as he thinketh in his heart, so is he...

Prayer is much like a frequency that God tunes into and listens to when we send out the vibrations of prayerful thought. I imagine God bending His ear towards us to listen when we approach the throne of grace in faith. Prayer is one of the things that can truly raise our vibration because it gives a sense of peace by leaving everything to His power and love.

Zephaniah 3:17 (NASB)
He will quiet you with His love.

God longs to empower us and the book of Timothy states,

2 Timothy 1:7 (KJV)
For God hath not given us the spirit of fear; but of power, and of love, and of a sound mind.

God has given us power! Do you remember what He said of the double-minded individual who waivers back and forth?

He said they were not of a sound mind and will not receive anything. They are like the waves of the sea, tossed back and forth between two minds that negate each other, so paralysis was the outcome. To be settled on an idea, a vision or a path is to be of sound mind, and that is when the blessings can flow. As Steven Pressfield stated, "When we commit to our vision or art or writing and do the work day after day, that is when heaven comes to our aid."

Philippians 4:6-7

Do not be anxious about anything, but in every situation, by prayer and petition, with thanksgiving, present your requests to God. ⁷ And the peace of God, which transcends all understanding, will guard your hearts and your minds in Christ Jesus.

God says to pray without anxiety, because anxiety does not truly acknowledge faith in the One to whom we pray. We are advised in everything, and in every situation, to pray. We are admonished to give thanks in the present tense, which also shows deep trust and faith. When we present our prayers and petitions with unwavering faith and trust, only then will the peace of God guard our hearts. This same sentiment is expressed in Proverbs chapter three because our view of circumstances is limited.

Proverbs 3:5-6 (NKJV)

*Trust in the Lord with all your heart,
And lean not on your own understanding;
⁶ In all your ways acknowledge Him,
And He shall direct your paths.*

We are to keep acknowledging the Lord and He will guide us. We have to get out of the way and let go, and let God take the lead. Charles Spurgeon says that the promises of God are like decrees and, like a decree, it shall be done.

Mark 11:24

Therefore I tell you, whatever you ask for in prayer, believe that you have received it, and it will be yours.

Charles Spurgeon says this Scripture verse has something to do with faith in miracles, but he really believes it has more to do with the miracle of faith. This Scripture states, *"believe that you have received it."* There has to be something definite which you pray for. Clarity is essential, along with earnest desire and unflinching faith. Charles Spurgeon also says, "You do not have to ransack the Bible for the right words—just say what you want, get to the point. It does not matter if it is money or a business or some great vision for something huge. Just say it!" No fine oratory is needed, just the words that are yours and yours alone. Make a straight aim at what you want and say, "Give me, Lord, the desires of my heart." Pray with earnest desire because Charles Spurgeon says, "Cold prayers ask for a denial." Pray the emotionalized prayer like the emotionalized thinking from the heart. There is a verse that states, "The effectual fervent prayer of a righteous man availeth much." (James 5:16, KJV) *Fervent* means of passionate intensity. I repeat: "Cold prayers die on the lips," says Charles Spurgeon.

There is a story of the ancient Greek philosopher, Socrates, who wanted to share the secret of success with his student Plato. One day, as they walked along a beach, Socrates asked Plato to walk into the water to about shoulder depth. Socrates then began to hold Plato under the water as he twisted and fought for air till he almost passed out. The angered Plato came around and accused Socrates of trying to kill him! Socrates said that was not his aim at all; rather, his aim was to teach Plato that when he desired knowledge as much as he desired breath, then he would have it.

That same principle can be applied to anything that we want to achieve. It truly has to be a burning desire of passionate intensity. If it is not, we will all too easily give up and never achieve the dream. That is the quality of prayer that moves mountains! Charles

Spurgeon calls prayer the mighty weapon that we have allowed to rust.

There is a portion of Scripture about the prayer of someone named Jabez. Bruce Wilkinson wrote the book entitled *The Prayer of Jabez*. Millions of copies of this book have been sold.

1 Chronicles 4:9-10 (NKJV)

Now Jabez was more honorable than his brothers, and his mother called his name Jabez, saying, "Because I bore him in pain." ¹⁰ And Jabez called on the God of Israel saying, "Oh, that You would bless me indeed, and enlarge my territory, that Your hand would be with me, and that You would keep me from evil, that I may not cause pain!" So God granted him what he requested.

This portion of the Bible is taken from a long list recording the genealogy of the Israelites. This list goes on for nine full chapters. In the midst of the seemingly endless list of names, the prayer of Jabez is recorded. It states that Jabez was more honourable than his brothers, which may imply that he was a man of prayer. He may have received less than his brothers or been shunned for his name, which was not a name of blessing, but one of pain.

Throughout all the shortcomings of his life, his dependence remained on God. He cried out to God to bless him *indeed!* He wanted his territory enlarged. He also asked God to keep His hand of protection upon him. Jabez cried out to God. Crying out implies that he implored God fervently and passionately. God granted what he requested. Imagine nine chapters of names listed, and only one prayer is recorded! God calls this man, who prays to be blessed, more honourable than his brothers. Is prayer the rusty weapon at your feet?

Prayer is a weapon of spiritual warfare. So please remember God is Spirit or energy. Everything is given life by spiritual energy. Scripture says you have been created in God's image in the first chapter of Genesis. He put a bit of heaven within you, in your magnificent energy powerhouse, which is your brain. When you express your desire in prayer to God, you are changing the vibration of the things not yet seen and not yet formed. Everything is composed of energy and vibrations. Prayer sends into the universe a vibration that raises your frequency to higher levels. Almost magically and magnetically, you have the ability to attract exactly what you envision. God says you do not have because you do not ask.

Our electrically charged brain is transmitting constantly and, if we come near to God, He tunes into us and comes near to us. If your prayer is weak, cold and inconsistent, it is of little impact. However, when you focus on your vision and enter into a private place—which the Bible calls a prayer closet—you can pray in earnestness of heart. This very action allows that mighty, creative power of the Spirit to change the energy around you and bring into form that which you seek to achieve. God asks, if anything is too hard for Him. The answer is no; not one thing. The Scriptures say He can do exceedingly abundantly more than all we ask. His thoughts and ways are so far above our own limited reasoning. If you base your prayers only on what you can comprehend, you will limit what the God of the impossible can do for you. Make your prayers big and make them bold. Scripture states open your mouth wide and He will fill it. Your prayers are His delight. Imagine how delighted God will be if your prayers are great prayers, born of giant faith.

Proverbs 15:8 (NKJV)
The prayer of the upright is His delight.

Pick up your rusty weapon and pray; it delights the Lord. Ask, seek and knock, and the door shall be opened. You shall be heard, since there is nothing too difficult for Him. It may not be as grand as a light bulb or a telephone, but your prayer will still be precious to Him. It will be His delight that you took time to ask in faith.

He longs to show Himself strong on your behalf. He longs to be a Father whom you can trust and depend on. He gave you a spirit of creative power, and wants you to live free of anxiety and fear in the power of His Spirit of love and unwavering faith.

Jeremiah 29:11-13

For I know the plans I have for you," declares the Lord, "plans to prosper you and not to harm you, plans to give you hope and a future. [12] Then you will call on me and come and pray to me, and I will listen to you. [13] You will seek me and find me when you seek me with all your heart."

Delight yourself in the Lord and He will give you the desires of your heart, because you are treasured. Revelation states that God saves your prayers in bowls. If your prayers are precious, then, like a loving father, He longs to give you what you want, if it is the best thing for you. However, there is another force at work in this world which will do everything in its power to keep you from ever achieving your dreams. Shall we continue to find out what this power is?

Chapter 5

THE POWER OF FAITH
AND HOPE

Ephesians 6:12

For our struggle is not against flesh and blood, but against the rulers, against the authorities, against the powers of this dark world and against the spiritual forces of evil in the heavenly realms.

Isaiah 40:31

*... those who hope in the Lord
will renew their strength.
They will soar on wings like eagles;
they will run and not grow weary,
they will walk and not be faint.*

In the last chapter we saw that prayer is a weapon. Have you ever thought of the concept of spiritual warfare in your life? If you scan world events, there certainly seems to be a force that is cruel, murderous and devoid of anything that is good. If the fruit of the Spirit is love, then where does the spirit of hate come from?

One reference in Scripture that I can think of tells us to hate what is evil and cling to what is good.

Romans 12:9

Love in Action
Love must be sincere. Hate what is evil;
cling to what is good.

While God longs for our best, there is a counter-force lurking to ensure failure, suffering and lack. There are many Scriptures that encourage us to be prepared to face this enemy, called the devil, who is spoken of in the Bible. He is likened to a roaring lion, looking for someone whom he can devour. I do not want to put too much focus on this evil force that longs to defeat us; however, I do want you to be aware that it can be what keeps you stuck in fear and lack of achievement. This evil force wants you to remain ineffective.

Napolean Hill wrote a book called *Outwitting the Devil.* There is a recording of it on YouTube. It is written like an interview. The essence of its message is that the most powerful influence of this malevolent spirit is to keep us drifting. Drifting alone will defeat us because there is no focus and no destination, clarity or vision. Drifting is sufficient to diffuse any power we may have within us and is enough to destroy all accomplishments. It is the force that will keep us from trying again, or at least trying with all that it takes for success.

Just think of a piece of wood floating aimlessly on the water. What does it do? It is much like the double-minded individual who is considered unstable in the Scriptures. The piece of wood is tossed on the waves, back and forth, aimless and without course. It may end up on the shore, but it would end up there without any effort of its own. Sometimes we look around and wonder how we got to where we are in our life, which is not where we wanted to be at all. Our uncharted course has taken us so far from where we hoped we would be. Drifting is energy of a low vibration, without determined goals, outcomes or success.

In the book, *The War of Art*, Steven Pressfield describes this enemy of our every endeavour as Resistance. He has graciously allowed me to quote his work, which I so love.

"Most of us live two lives. The life we live and the unlived life within us. Between the two stands Resistance.

Have you ever brought home a treadmill and let it gather dust in the attic? Have you ever quit a diet, a course of yoga, a meditation practice? Have you ever bailed out on a call to embark upon a spiritual practice, dedicate yourself to a humanitarian calling, or commit your life to the service of others? Have you ever wanted to be a mother, a doctor, an advocate for the weak and helpless; to run for office, crusade for the planet, campaign for world peace, or to preserve the environment? Late at night you have experienced a vision of the person you might become, the work you could accomplish, the realized being you were meant to be. Are you a writer who doesn't write, or an entrepreneur who never starts a venture? Then you know what Resistance is.

Resistance is the most toxic force on the planet...To yield to Resistance deforms our spirit. It stunts us and makes us less than we are and were born to be. If you believe in God (and I do) you must declare Resistance evil, for it prevents us from achieving the life God intended when He endowed each of us with our own unique genius. Genius is a Latin word; the Romans used it to denote an inner spirit, holy and inviolable, which watches over us, guiding us to our calling.

As powerful as is our soul's call to realization, so potent are the forces of Resistance arrayed against it...

Is this what it takes? Do we have to stare death in the face to make us stand up and confront Resistance? Does Resistance have to cripple and disfigure our lives before we wake up to its existence? How many of us have become drunks and drug addicts, developed tumours and neuroses, succumbed to painkillers, gossip, and compulsive cell phone use, simply because we don't do the thing that our hearts, our inner genius, is calling us to? Resistance defeats us."

How do we fight Resistance or the one that would keep us in a state of inertia? We try to think positively, repeat our declarations, study our vision boards or get daily inspirational quotes via email. We spend thousands or billions collectively, on personal development, trying to flip the switch to self-actualization in order to quiet that call on our lives that is not being fulfilled. I know, because I have done it all!

Steven Pressfield says the solution is to "just do the work; sit down and do the work." Day after day, do what you are avoiding. The Bible says to go the extra mile. Do not sit on the starting line, but run the first mile, and then the next, and then the one after that. Vince Lombardi, who was one of the greatest football coaches, said, "I have never known a really successful person who deep in his heart did not understand the grind, the daily discipline required to win." Step out in faith, because faith is not faith until you take that first step. Grind fear under the heel of faith in God, who is looking to empower you because you are created in His image. You were created with a brain, and a will, and power to do anything that you set your heart and your mind to do! It is the daily disciplines that change things. God says that His people perish for lack of a vision. Please do not let your vision perish for a lack of faith and action.

Robin Sharma says: "The activity you are most avoiding contains your biggest opportunity."

1 Corinthians 16:13-14

Be on your guard; stand firm in the faith; be courageous; be strong. Do everything in love.

Hebrews 11:1

Faith in Action
Now faith is confidence in what we hope for and assurance about what we do not see.

2 Corinthians 5:7

For we live by faith and not by sight.

Resistance and drifting defeats us, but faith empowers us if we will step out and take inspired action. Doesn't "inspired action" sound lofty, of high frequency and vibration, and filled with the guidance of the Spirit? I most certainly think so. Let me repeat what Nikola Tesla said: "The gift of mental power comes from God, Divine Being, and if we concentrate our minds on that truth, we become in tune with that great power." In order to be in tune with this great power, we must have faith, for we cannot please God or go to Him if we do not believe that He exists.

Hebrews 11:6

And without faith it is impossible to please God, because anyone who comes to him must believe that he exists and that he rewards those who earnestly seek him.

Would you consider yourself a person of faith? We live so much in the reality of only what we can see and touch. We love to say to one another, "Prove it to me and then I will believe it." But that is as the world sees. It completely leaves out the realm of the supernatural, miracles and the divine. The things of the Spirit speak to the statement, "Believe it and I will prove it to you."

We learned from the chapter discussing the universe and the brain, that the billions of vibrating atoms are filled with waves of energy. It is said that the language of communication is electricity, or unseen energy. Bob Proctor and others call this energy "Spirit." We know this energy exists when we turn on a light bulb. Electrical energy is unseen, but we have faith in its existence every time we flip the light switch, short of a power failure. People believe in ghosts, aliens, and mediums which are all unseen, yet so many refuse to accept or believe in God! They are faithless when it comes to God. They would much rather embrace the alignment of stars in the sky, tarot cards, charms, Ouija boards, etc. The Bible was written over 1500 years from beginning to end and forms one cohesive book of great wisdom, which speaks of the reality of a personal, loving God who longs to be in relationship with people.

Why is it that so many struggle with lack of faith in the Divine Creator? Still others have only a nominal acknowledgement of the possibility of the existence of God? Many people consider themselves rational, intelligent thinkers. They perceive themselves as independent and self-reliant. I have heard so many tell me faith is simply a crutch for the weak. They say that they are not weak, so faith in God is not necessary in their lives. Faith is belief in God whether you are weak or strong! My faith is greatly strengthened by daily reading of the Word of God, which for me is the Bible. I know that as I matured in my faith, I have been able to truly, "Let go and let God." My faith has been the anchor that has held me through every storm of loss, grief, disease, heartache and disappointment. I do not know how I would have coped, if it were not for my faith. I have learned not to hold on to bitterness and anger, since the only one truly poisoned by holding on to these would be me. The Word says that allowing a root of bitterness to grow in our heart will defile every relationship, because it is within our heart that we feel and it is from the heart that we speak. Is it any wonder that the Bible tells us to forgive seventy times seven?

To be free in life, we are to live above our circumstances and not be defeated by them. The Bible tells us to cast all our burdens upon the Lord because He cares for us. We are admonished to get rid of everything that is negative. God wants us to be positive people who live in the spirit of love. The things that truly defeat us are emotions such as,

Galatians 5:20-21

...hatred, discord, jealousy, fits of rage, selfish ambition, dissensions, factions, envy, [and] drunkenness...

These qualities are offensive and they will keep you from the kingdom of blessing. They will also repel friends, family and business associates. They are feelings of such low vibration that the only people who could truly associate with someone like this would be those of the same mindset, which would only magnify the destructive effect of these negative energies.

Remember that experience that I had at the Holy Spirit Conference, where I experienced the tender love of God in a vision? Well, once the vision had lifted, I felt the Presence still very much upon me, and the slightest complaint or judgement was so wounding to that Divine Heart of love. God says that if we truly live in relationship with His Spirit, we will exhibit the attributes or fruit of the Divine Spirit.

Galatians 5:22-23

But the fruit of the Spirit is love, joy, peace, forbearance, kindness, goodness, faithfulness, [23] gentleness and self-control.

God says there is nothing that can be said against these characteristics. These qualities are positive, and of high vibration. They can only attract more of the same into our lives.

I love the precepts of the Word of God. They have become my friend and have taught me about the sweetest love there is. God asks us to take off the old self, be renewed in the attitude of our minds, and put on the new self. The new self is created to be like

God in true righteousness. (Colossians 3)God also admonishes us to not let any unwholesome talk come out of our mouths, but only speak what is helpful for building others up, according to their needs, so that the words may be of benefit to those who listen. One of my favourite portions of Scripture tells us not to grieve the Holy Spirit. It says:

Ephesians 4:29-32

Do not let any unwholesome talk come out of your mouths, but only what is helpful for building others up according to their needs, that it may benefit those who listen. [30] And do not grieve the Holy Spirit of God, with whom you were sealed for the day of redemption. [31] Get rid of all bitterness, rage and anger, brawling and slander, along with every form of malice. [32] Be kind and compassionate to one another, forgiving each other, just as in Christ God forgave you.

I listened to an interview with Sir Richard Branson about his business and all that he had achieved. At the end of the interview, he was asked to give one piece of advice to people starting out in business. He answered without hesitation, "See the best in people." To see the best is to be positive and to live on a high vibration. To see the best in everything is not to see lack, but to see goodness, possibilities and abundance. See the best, seek the best, speak the best, think the best, and trust the best will come to you. Stay in that very high vibration of faith and trust. Stay committed to your dream, desire or vision. God says there is no lack. Jesus came so we would have life and have it abundantly. (John 10:10) Winston Churchill stated: "A pessimist sees the difficulty in every opportunity; an optimist sees the opportunity in every difficulty."

God wants us to have enough faith to live in the goodness of all that is positive. The Scriptures exhort us to "Rejoice in the Lord always" and then it is repeated again, "Rejoice!" The joy of the Lord is our strength. Joy is such a positive word of magnetic attraction. Just thinking of deep joy in someone makes me smile. Joy is so much more than happiness. To seek God earnestly is to have faith and reach toward Him with fervent, passionate prayer. Remember "Cold prayers of little faith die on the lips," as Spurgeon said, and "beg a refusal." Revelation states that we are either hot or cold for God. It is the lukewarm, dispassionate faith that is so distasteful to Him. It is so distasteful that He would rather spit the lukewarm person out.

Revelation 3:15-16

I know your deeds, that you are neither cold nor hot.
I wish you were either one or the other! [16] So, because you
are lukewarm—neither hot nor cold—I am about to spit
you out of my mouth.

Is it any wonder why so many lukewarm, watered-down churches are closing their doors? The passion for faith, prayer, and love for the Lord cooled years ago. He left the building! The empty traditions of bake sales, rummage sales, and coffee chats with a teaspoon of Scripture diminishes the power of scripture into more like taking a dose of medicine. Those old pews once filled with the faithful are almost empty. The churches that are bursting with people are alive with faith, joy, music and deep truth from the Scriptures being preached from the pulpit. You can see the churches and ministries that have vision and massive faith, because their impact reaches far into the communities or towns where they are located, and even beyond into the world.

A daily newspaper did a three page article on a church pastor who said she was an atheist and yet the members had asked her to stay on. God is not wanted there! The people there left all the power of faith; they no longer know the voice of Scripture or what it has to say. Their vibration is now too low; they have turned away. They have become deaf to "the Way".

Isaiah 53:6 (NKJV)

*...we like sheep have gone astray; We have turned, every one,
to his own way...*

Billy Graham was asked what you have to do to lose your faith. His profound answer was, "Nothing, it will die all on its own." Faith is sustained much like a relationship. Times of prayer, reading the Bible and meditation builds our faith, just like taking time to be with someone and sharing with them, strengthens friendships and family ties. Think of the church that embraced the atheist pastor. Their void was filled with teaching of another kind.

Ephesians 3:20-21

*Now to him who is able to do immeasurably more than
all we ask or imagine, according to his power that is
at work within us, 21 to him be glory in the church and
in Christ Jesus throughout all generations,
for ever and ever! Amen.*

Rejoice, and I say it again, rejoice that we have a God who is able to do so much more than we could ever ask or imagine. How does God do it? This verse says that it is through the power that is at work within us. It is the same power that raised Christ from the dead. We have been given the Spirit of power, and love and of a sound mind. Who did God say was not of sound mind? It was the ones who could not make up their mind. They could not remain steady and faithful to the dream or desire within their heart. This is why we are cautioned over and over again not to fear or be anxious, but to live in steadfast faith in the One who can do exceedingly abundantly more than we could ever hope or dream of. Our thoughts are so small in comparison to God's. So often fear overrides faith. Do not let it! Let your faith override fear. Get a clear vision of what you want and take a giant step toward the picture in your mind; it may have been put there by the Spirit of God to be achieved by you alone! It is your very own destiny seeking fulfillment.

Isaiah 55:9

"For my thoughts are not your thoughts,
neither are your ways my ways,"
declares the Lord.
"As the heavens are higher than the earth,
so are my ways higher than your ways
and my thoughts than your thoughts"

God can do so much more than we can imagine or dream of. It is the dreamers who are able to access this great power because they are empowered with imagination. They are not restricted by human reasoning.

The LORD wants you to come before Him in every situation, with thanksgiving, and present your requests in faith and trust that your prayer has been heard. It is then that we are to rest in faith in order to receive the peace that passes understanding. Fretting and fussing is never going to give you peace, but steadfast faith will. Even in the worst of times, we can hang on to the fact that God understands our sorrows and pain. We are eternal beings and for those of us who are spiritual, we know this world is not our home; we are just passing through. The Bible describes all the troubles we face in this world as "light and momentary". Faith gives us the fortitude to understand that, in this world, we will have trouble and trials. However, if we do not lean on our own understanding, but constantly remember God in an attitude of praying without ceasing, He will direct our paths. He will be an ever-present source of comfort and strength. Scripture says you will find God when you seek Him with all your heart.

We can change circumstances from what is, to what can be. We do this through our words, our thoughts, and our prayers. Keep looking above and beyond the present circumstances. Make your affirmations and your prayers of faith present tense with gratitude.

This shows immense faith in the goodness of the universe, which is filled with the Spirit of God.

Bob Proctor states, "Make the decision and the money will come." This quote has been my inspiration to do so many things that I otherwise would not have done. It has never failed me. I believe that whatever you have decided on will be achieved. Make your decisions with faith in the positive outcome you seek, and it will come into form. Take advantage of the great power of God and do not make your goal too small. I love the statement by Bob Proctor: "If you know how to reach your goal, then the goal is not big enough."

Remember, the Bible says to trust the Lord and do not rely on your own understanding, but always acknowledge the One who is vastly greater than you, and then your paths will be directed by God. In order to maintain a high vibration and be positively magnetized, we must be positive and strive to say things in a positive manner. For example, do not say, "I do not want to be late," but say instead, "I will be on time." It is small, but what we speak we attract. What we focus on expands, so make your focus positive; keep your thoughts and words uplifting,

Philippians 4:8-9

Finally, brothers and sisters, whatever is true, whatever is noble, whatever is right, whatever is pure, whatever is lovely, whatever is admirable—if anything is excellent or praiseworthy—think about such things. Whatever you have learned or received or heard from me, or seen in me—put it into practice. And the God of peace will be with you.

There is no room for defeated despondency. We are to think about what is true, noble, right, pure, lovely, admirable, excellent and praiseworthy. Our thoughts are to be those that are altogether lovely and, in so being, they will be thoughts that empower us. Defeated thoughts are not from the Lord, so let your hope be in the Lord and let His power be your very own.

Ephesians 3:20-21

Now to him who is able to do immeasurably more than all we ask or imagine, according to his power that is at work within us, to him be glory in the church and in Christ Jesus throughout all generations, for ever and ever! Amen.

The *Amen* of this verse seems to make it sound as if what we want to achieve is done just like that, and, in some cases, it is achieved just like that! But sometimes it takes a long time, and that is when faith can waver and we might want to give up. That is when hope steps in. When I first started to think of faith and hope, it was difficult to express how they were different. Like twins, who are very much the same, they are also different. Faith and hope are necessary to achieve things that take long-term effort or extended times of waiting.

When we decide that we are going to achieve something, we do not say, "I hope it happens." Hope, in that context, is not sure. Faith is much stronger in contrast. Faith is present tense, in the sense that we believe that the thing is already done, and we are giving thanks before it even appears. When you have faith to achieve something, but it does not seem to be happening, hope is what keeps us going when resolve falters.

Hebrews 6:19

...We have this hope as an anchor for the soul, firm and secure...

Dr. Barbara L. Fredrickson argues that "hope comes into its own when crisis looms, opening us to new creative possibilities." Frederickson argues that with great need comes an unusually wide range of ideas, as well as such positive emotions as happiness and joy, courage, and empowerment, drawn from four different areas of one's self: from a cognitive, psychological, social, or physical perspective. Hopeful people are "'like the little engine that could, [because] they keep telling themselves "I think I can, I think I can".'"

Such positive thinking bears fruit when based on a realistic sense of optimism, not on a naive "false hope". (Wikipeadia)

When faith is being challenged, hope is like the second runner in a relay race. As faith falters, hope digs in with determination to find a way and to trust that the end goal will be achieved. God admonishes us to keep on asking, keep on searching and keep on knocking. Scripture states then, the door will be opened.

I love the famous speech Winston Churchill gave to encourage the students of a school during the Second World War. "I am addressing myself to the school—surely from this period of ten months this is the lesson: *never give in, never give in, never, never, never, never-in nothing, great or small, large or petty—never give in except to convictions of honour and good sense.* Never yield to force; never yield to the apparently overwhelming might of the enemy." I am sure that this caused hope to rise in the hearts of the students as the imminent danger to their island home loomed so close.

As the bombing of Britain continued, Winston Churchill conquered fear and inspired hope in the people with his speech, "We shall not flag or fail, we shall go on to the end. We shall fight them on the seas and the oceans. We shall fight them with growing confidence and growing strength in the air. We shall defend our island, whatever the cost may be. We shall fight on the beaches. We shall fight on the landing grounds. We shall fight in the fields and in the streets. We shall fight in the hills. We shall never surrender!"

The only outcome to be considered by the people was victory! Defeat and failure was not an option, even as the mighty nations of Europe fell before their eyes. Scripture states,

Romans 5:3-5

And not only this, but we also exult in our tribulations, knowing that tribulation brings about perseverance; 4 and perseverance, proven character; and proven character, hope; 5 and hope does not disappoint, because the love of God has been poured out within our hearts through the Holy Spirit who was given to us.

We can see that if we persevere through the challenges that beset us, stand firm in faith, unwavering in hope, and do not give up, our character grows! As Steven Pressfield has mentioned, as we work faithfully the "Muse" will come to our aid. Scripture states we will feel the love of God's Spirit poured into our hearts. God is the "Our Father" or Abba who comes to our aid and assists of our accomplishments. He says "I will strengthen you and help you" in Isaiah 41:10.

The title verse for hope in this chapter is,

Isaiah 40:31

Those who hope in the Lord
will renew their strength.
They will soar on wings like eagles;
they will run and not grow weary,
they will walk and not be faint.

So do not struggle alone, but depend on the power of the Spirit of God to strengthen and help you. Continue praying, asking and searching. Think of your dream continually. Implant it deep into your mind and subconscious. All you need is a clear vision and burning desire, matched with effort. The way will be shown!

Romans 15:13

May the God of hope fill you with all joy and peace as you
trust in him, so that you may overflow with hope by
the power of the Holy Spirit.

There is faith, hope and love, but the greatest of these is love! So on we go!

Chapter 6

THE POWER OF LOVE
AND GRATITUDE

1 John 4:8

*Whoever does not love does not know God,
because God is love.*

1 Thessalonians 5:16-18

*Rejoice always, pray continually, give thanks in all
circumstances; for this is God's will for you in Christ Jesus.*

To know God, we must have love in our hearts. Previously, I mentioned being in resonance and in the right frequency to tune into God. The first verse above states if you do not have love in your heart, then you do not know God. We all have love in our hearts, but how does that love get tuned into God?

James 4:8

Come near to God and he will come near to you.

We see in this verse the beginning of relationship. God wants to be near to you, but He will never force His love or His will upon your life. When I was young, I was intrigued by a dusty, old print in a junk shop. The print was in the muted shades of an old painting. It was a picture of Jesus in a wild, overgrown garden, knocking on a door. The door was old and rustic, and the hinges were rusted. In the dark of night, Jesus held a lamp in one hand and with the other He knocked on the door. In the glow of the lamp, He was leaning forward as He knocked. His gentle face seemed to express warmth and kindness. There was no doorknob on the door; it was a door which could only be opened from the inside. That old, great painting was portraying the famous Bible verse from Revelation 3:20.

Revelation 3:20

Here I am! I stand at the door and knock. If anyone hears my voice and opens the door, I will come in and eat with that person, and they with me.

I have never really taken note of an exclamation mark in Scripture before, but I am intrigued with the one in this verse. As God knocks on the door, He exclaims His presence. To *exclaim* is to call out, to yell, to announce, or to shout out. God wants to be heard as He knocks. Remember, He is the God who whispers. We see the tender heart of God when He speaks in a soft whisper to the depressed and frightened Elijah in the cave. But here, at the closed door, He proclaims His presence loudly. This door symbolizes the door to your very own heart, and the Lord really wants to be heard. He seeks to make Himself known and, as we have seen, He is seeking those who can hear Him, because they are in resonance with Him and have hearts that are searching for Him. He is carrying a lamp which symbolizes that He is bringing light. Scripture states, He is the light of the world and His Word which is the Bible is described as a lamp that dispels the darkness!

John 8:12

When Jesus spoke again to the people, he said, "I am the light of the world. Whoever follows me will never walk in darkness, but will have the light of life."

Psalm 119:105 (KJV)

*Thy word is a lamp unto my feet, and
a light unto my path.*

There is a parable of the good shepherd who lost a sheep, and He leaves the other ninety-nine in order to find that one lost sheep. If you are feeling lost or lonely in search of something, but you do not know what, please know that the great heart of God is searching for you. He wants to be known by you! He says you will find Him when you search for Him with your whole heart.

I did that very thing decades ago when I felt something was missing in my life. It was a void that nothing could fill. I went on that great search, from church to church. I did not know what I was searching for until I felt prompted to attend a local church which God knew would share with me what I needed to hear. It was there that I heard the great gospel of Jesus, who had laid down His life on the cross as a guilt offering to purchase my pardon. Everything within me was energized and my whole being was in a battle to embrace or reject this truth. It was the truth that Christ had died on the cross to pay the price of holy justice. He paid the death penalty for the whole world, to cover every failure, every mistake and every crime. The question for you is: Can you embrace this truth for yourself by opening the door of your heart to the Great God of love?

Hebrews 1:3

*The Son is the radiance of God's glory and the exact
representation of his being, sustaining all things by his
powerful word. After he had provided purification for sins,
he sat down at the right hand of the Majesty in heaven.*

God is knocking on the door of your heart, asking you to let Him in so He can share your life. He longs to dine with you and have you dine with Him. He wants to hear your every prayer and rejoice in your every triumph. He will be the anchor of your life in every storm, as He has been in mine. Yes, He knows you will have trouble in this world, but He is the one who says to cast your burdens upon Him because He cares for you. His Word, the Bible, is where you will come to know this great loving, longing, forgiving heart. He says the Word of God will be the light that guides your every path.

The deep truths of His word can only be truly understood by the spirit-filled sincerely seeking heart. The Bible is called the sword of the Holy Spirit, and it can become the source of deep wisdom and understanding in your life. I am struck that it is called the sword of the Holy Spirit but, in order to become that sword, it must be read and studied. I would say it must be loved. The more we read the Bible, the sweeter and more powerful it will become. Jesus also said:

John 14:6

I am the way and the truth and the life.

Jesus said that He is the truth. Nikola Tesla stated: "The gift of mental power comes from God, Divine Being, and if we concentrate our minds on that truth, we become in tune with this great power." "Men stumble over the truth from time to time, but most pick themselves up and hurry off as if nothing happened," was a profound statement made by Winston Churchill.

Scripture likens us to earthen vessels which can be filled with the power of God. Remember your power is within your magnificent mind. In that mind, you are given the ability to choose success or failure. You are plugged into the power of the Almighty, because your mind is seamlessly connected to the One who says that nothing is too hard for Him. Your mind is the one thing that you have total control of; so, with your mind you choose the outcome and the results in your life.

God is Spirit; the Spirit is love, and it is present everywhere. As Ephesians 4 says, it fills the whole universe. The universe is filled with power and endless energy that is never static but is a mass of vibrating atoms of waves of energy.

Ephesians 4:10

He who descended is the very one who ascended higher than all the heavens, in order to fill the whole universe.

Send your thoughts into this unseen energy or Divine Spirit and you will impress what you want upon it. If you desire something with all your heart, endless thoughts, expectancy and effort, your desire will be manifested, for it is a universal law. It has to, because the Law of the Perpetual Transmutation of Energy is bringing it into form, and then the Law of Attraction will bring it to you. We are like magnets, and magnets possess two ends. One is positive and the other is negative. They are polar opposites, and you can choose whether what you want in your life is positive or negative. Use your mind wisely for it holds the key to joy and abundance or sadness and lack.

God delights in your prayers! Not the lukewarm, whatever, sort of prayers, but the passionate, heartfelt, sincere ones. Make your prayers big and bold, filled with creative imagination, and sincerely believe. You will increase the delight of God by your great faith! Remember that God gives according to His vast immeasurable love, but we receive only according to the measure of our faith. I repeat; God has immense love for you and longs to be gracious and strong on your behalf. He is love and will give according to that love. The only limitation for what you receive is the size of your faith and how much you ask for. Do not forget to go the extra mile in order to achieve your desire, though this is not required in all circumstances. If there is nothing you can do but pray, then earnestly pray, but if you need to take action, then take action—consistent, determined and dedicated action.

Let's see what the Word says about love, and read the chapter that is chosen to be read at the majority of wedding services.

1 Corinthians 13:1-8, 13

If I speak in the tongues of men or of angels, but do not have love, I am only a resounding gong or a clanging cymbal. ² If I have the gift of prophecy and can fathom all mysteries and all knowledge, and if I have a faith that can move mountains, but do not have love, I am nothing. ³ If I give all I possess to the poor and give over my body to hardship that I may boast, but do not have love, I gain nothing.⁴ Love is patient, love is kind. It does not envy, it does not boast, it is not proud. ⁵ It does not dishonour others, it is not self-seeking, it is not easily angered, it keeps no record of wrongs. ⁶ Love does not delight in evil but rejoices with the truth. ⁷ It always protects, always trusts, always hopes, always perseveres.⁸ Love never fails…
¹³ And now these three remain: faith, hope and love. But the greatest of these is love.

These lovely qualities of love are also much like the fruit of the Spirit from Galatians 5, which we are to exhibit if we are in resonance and on the same frequency as God, who is love.

Love is:
Patient
Kind
Does not boast
Not Rude
Not Self Seeking
Not Easily Angered
Keeps No Records of Wrong
Does Not Delight in Evil
Rejoices with the Truth
Always Protects
Always Trusts

Galatians 5:22-23

But the fruit of the Spirit is love, joy, peace, forbearance [patience], kindness, goodness, faithfulness, [23] gentleness and self-control. Against such things there is no law.

The Fruit of the Holy Spirit:

Love
Joy
Peace
Patience
Kindness
Goodness
Faithfulness
Gentleness
Self-Control

Philippians 4:8

Finally, brothers and sisters, whatever is true, whatever is noble, whatever is right, whatever is pure, whatever is lovely, whatever is admirable—if anything is excellent or praiseworthy—think about such things.

Think About What Is:

True
Noble
Right
Pure
Lovely
Admirable
Excellent
Praiseworthy

All of the words in these three lists capture just how positive our thoughts, feelings and character qualities are to be. Such a God of love and purity can only want the best for us. As God thinks loving thoughts and sentiments about us, so we are to be like-minded toward others. The Law of Attraction causes us to reap what we sow or to receive what we give. As we think, speak and act toward others, we, in turn, will receive the same in response. Hence, we are admonished not to judge others, for as we judge, we will be judged, and with the measure we use (greed or generosity), it will be measured to us. That is the Law of Cause and Effect.

When we tune into the frequency of the Spirit, which is present everywhere in the universe, and we grasp how wide and long and high and deep the love of the Spirit of God is, then we will be filled with the fullness of God. His love is fully towards us. It took me a long time of reading the Scriptures to begin to understand the fullness of how tender and, in many instances, how wounded God is by our lack of love for Him in return. He wants you to know the fullness of His love. The Apostle Paul knelt in prayer before the Lord in order that we would know this love and all the power that comes with it. When there is fullness of love, there is freedom from fear. God's perfect love casts out fear, and love also covers a multitude of sins! Scripture states:

1 John 4:18

There is no fear in love. But perfect love drives out fear, because fear has to do with punishment. The one who fears is not made perfect in love.

Once the knowledge of this love has filled our hearts, we can stop being afraid. We are free to trust this Mighty Love. We can go boldly before the throne of grace and present our petitions without fear and with thanksgiving. God says in the Bible, if we give good gifts to our children, then how much more will our Father in heaven, who loves us with His very life, give to us.

Many people are achieving much without faith, yet can you

imagine how many secrets would be revealed to them if they came in faith to the power that is known to the great dreamers of this world? To become in tune with God is to be in resonance with His frequency of creative power.

We see that the lists which describe the qualities of love— the fruit of the Spirit and the thoughts we are to think—are all positive. All of these words make us feel good. Feelings are a good way to test our vibration and what we are attracting. Think about all the areas of your life. If you are feeling bad about money, health or business, then you are only going to attract more of the same to your life. If you are feeling good and giving love, then you are positive and your vibration attracts more positive energy to yourself. So, monitor your feelings since they are like a barometer, indicating whether you are attracting or repelling what you want. There are things you can do to change your vibration. Remember God created you, and you have created and are creating the rest in your life.

I find it amazing how quickly my feelings can change. I can be on top of the world one day, embracing all that is good, and then slide into a pity party the next. I always wonder if I am erasing all that has been positive. I have learned that each day comes with its own vibration, so we must make every effort to silence negativity because it repels what we are seeking.

Think of the word *"enthusiasm"*. What comes to mind? I think of energy, joy and happiness, great smiles, passion and love. I have a friend who is constantly filled with enthusiasm. She is a little deaf, but does everything with unabashed enthusiasm! She speaks a little louder, laughs a little longer and hugs a little harder. Connie is filled with unabashed love for people, babies and God. She bounds into a room, and when she does, you know she has arrived, for her positive, loving energy fills the room. She needs to be around people, and people gravitate to her and all her love is returned to her. You just have to mention her name and it brings a smile to everyone's face. There is nothing lukewarm about her and her effervescent personality spreads joy wherever she goes.

Enthusiasm is magnetic, powerfully uplifting and inspiring. *Enthusiasm* comes from the root of *en theos* which means in God. Now examine how God considers those who are lukewarm. I remind you, He wants to spit out anything that is lukewarm! If we love God, we will be enthusiastic for Him. God wants our love to be complete, not half-hearted.

Mark 12:30-31

'Love the Lord your God with all your <u>heart</u> and with all your <u>soul</u> and with all your <u>mind</u> and with all your <u>strength</u>.' [31] The second is this: 'Love your neighbour as yourself.' There is no commandment greater than these.

God wants us to love Him with everything we've got and to give Him our very best. There is nothing lukewarm about the intensity of the relationship that He wants to share with us. He also wants us to love one another. We are to seek Him first, before all things, because that is where wisdom, guidance and blessings come from. He says to do everything as if you were working for God and He will reward you for your efforts. To be profoundly effective in our lives is glorifying to God. He wants our success in all things and in all areas. He has given us the power to achieve anything we truly desire through our thoughts, determination and action. Ralph Waldo Emerson said, "Nothing great was ever achieved without *enthusiasm*." The American steel magnate, Charles Schwab, declared, "You can succeed at almost anything for which you have unlimited *enthusiasm*."

Colossians 3:23-24

Whatever you do, work at it with all your heart, as working for the Lord, not for human masters, [24] since you know that you will receive an inheritance from the Lord as a reward.

Enthusiasm for an idea, a dream or a vision will keep you going, and you will not grow weary as you trust in the Lord. Scripture states the power of God will lift you up, as if you were on the wings of an eagle. As we run the race before us in life, let us not forget the admonition to give thanks in all things! I repeat; give thanks in all circumstances! I wonder how endless gratitude would affect me and those I meet. When we say "Thank you," what does it do for others? It makes them feel appreciated, acknowledged and affirmed. We all need validation in our lives, and taking just a moment to say "Thank you" means so much to everyone who receives it. God is so wise. He knows that gratitude is powerful, not only when expressed to others, but especially to Him! When someone is grateful for what I have done or given, it truly warms my heart. The Scriptures say to rise in the morning and give thanks, and then give thanks again in the evening.

1 Thessalonians 5:16-18

Rejoice always, [17] pray continually, [18] give thanks in all circumstances; for this is God's will for you in Christ Jesus.

I first heard about a gratitude journal on the Oprah show. It seemed like a strange, but interesting idea. She interviewed several people who shared how the daily practice of writing down what they were thankful for made a significant positive difference in their lives. If I recall correctly, they found that much of their discontent disappeared. They felt more positive and had more energy. Oprah says that she kept a gratitude journal for a decade without fail. She would write five things that she was grateful for every day. Then life became very busy and the practise became sporadic. She found that having so much to do was less fulfilling and not as enjoyable. Oprah says she is now taking the time to write electronically, about the things that she is grateful for, even though she is just as busy. I realize, from Oprah, that focused gratitude is a counterweight to the endless daily challenges we face. Being grateful tips the scales of life in our favour. Remember what happens when we are in a positive vibration; the positive is magnified in our lives. The more we practise gratitude, the greater a habit it becomes. Practising gratitude is like strengthening a muscle. It is easy for the happy person to be grateful, but it really is the grateful person who is happy.

Gratitude is an attitude of life. Some people are never happy and complain about everything. They only see lack and vexation, then wonder why the same things continue to crop up in their lives. I know someone who has so much to be grateful for, but her thoughts are stuck in the past, where she experienced great material loss. No matter how I try to point out all the wonderful things that are good in her life now, the script in her mind is entrenched in negativity. No amount of encouragement can get her to acknowledge gratitude in the present. Some people just cannot say "Thank you," or see anything good. I realize that these people affect me by lowering my vibration so much, that I just cannot be in their presence for long. Beware of the company you keep because negative people will affect you negatively. So, let us raise a toast to the power of gratitude and acknowledge that the power of it can be transformational. Oprah Winfrey says, "Be thankful for what you have; you'll end up having more. If you concentrate on what you don't have, you will never, ever have enough."

Scripture says to give thanks in all things! It also says to forgive freely and often. So, turn the page and find out more on the power of forgiveness.

Chapter 7

THE POWER OF FORGIVENESS

Psalm 86:5

*You, Lord, are forgiving and good, abounding in love
to all who call to you.*

Forgiveness is the act of letting go of an offence or a payment owed. It is the wiping clean of the slate. Forgiveness is rooted in kindness and compassion. It gives the person a fresh start. In many ways, it is setting the offending person free from guilt, or punishment and shame. To truly forgive an offence, is to offer the hand of fellowship and set the person free from the obligation that is yet to be paid. Forgiveness lifts burdens and lightens the weight of the future on the person who has to make amends. Forgiveness is an act of grace that is not required but given nonetheless.

Did you know there is a difference between mercy and grace? Mercy is actually letting go of punishment deserved, and grace is extending kindness to those undeserving of it. We see in the chapter verse that God is abounding in love to all. He is the one who is forgiving and good. Scripture states we are to forgive others as we have been forgiven by God. There is a parable of a rich man who learned that his servant owed him much. The rich man forgave his servant a great debt. The servant then had someone else thrown into jail because they could not repay him a small debt. When the rich man heard of it, he was incensed, and had the servant sent to jail. The act of mercy which had been extended by the rich man was revoked due to the lack of mercy shown by the servant. Here we see the law of cause and effect. For every action there is a response or, as Scripture says, "we reap what we sow." As the servant threw the other poor man into jail, so he, in turn, was thrown into jail.

Scriptures mention that we are to be people of forgiveness, and Jesus was asked if seven times was sufficient to forgive someone. Jesus responded, "No." The disciple was informed that he was to forgive seventy times seven. We are not to hold onto offences but are to forgive others. In the ongoing act of forgiveness, we set ourselves free from becoming stuck in ever-growing bitterness. Have you ever met those who are irritated at everything and pick up insult and injury to their pride and self importance wherever they go? They have such toxic negative energy that it is depressing to be in their company. The bitterness touches everything they come in contact with.

Forgiveness is an attitude of letting things go, and moving on without magnifying every irritation and perceived slight. The act of forgiving gets stronger with use. I think forgiveness comes from a patient heart, filled with the spirit of love. Forgiveness comes from the root of love, and love covers a multitude of sins!

God loves us with infinite love, and He asks us to love Him with all that is within us, and to love others as we love ourselves. As God extends His loving heart to you, much like the rich man to his servant, then you are asked to do the same for others. In the last chapter, we talked about opening your heart to Jesus as He knocks on the door of your heart. Scripture states that, when you open your heart, God's love is poured into it through the Holy Spirit. This great love is released, when you choose faith in God.

God delights in your prayers. Micah 7:18 states that God delights to show mercy toward you. God is a holy, righteous God. He is a

God of justice. We have a system of justice in our society where the law breakers are sentenced to serve time for their robberies, drug use, murders or theft. If we have a system of justice, how much more will a holy, righteous God have one? In the Old Testament, the Israelites placed their hands on the head of a lamb or a goat and symbolically transferred their sins to the animal, which was then sacrificed in their place. Their sins were atoned for by the blood of the animal. This practice became only a ritual with little impact on the lives of those presenting their guilt offerings.

The Jewish people celebrate Passover to remember the great intervention of God to move Pharaoh to allow the people to leave Egypt, where they were slaves. In order to protect the people from the spirit of death, which was coming upon the land, the Israelites were instructed to apply the blood of a lamb to the doorframes of their homes, and to close the door. The spirit of death passed over every doorframe covered by the blood of the lamb. The Israelites were saved. The blood of the lamb is what saved them from death. After this miracle, Pharaoh finally let the people go. This exit from Egypt was called the Exodus.

Jesus is called the Lamb of God. God is merciful, but the sin or wrongdoing of the world is just too great to leave without some form of judgement. God, in His mercy, provided us with the way of forgiveness. Scripture verifies this in the two following verses:

1 Peter 3:18

For Christ also suffered once for sins, the righteous for the unrighteous, to bring you to God. He was put to death in the body but made alive in the Spirit.

Ephesians 2:8-9

For it is by grace you have been saved, through faith—and this is not from yourselves, it is the gift of God— ⁹ not by works, so that no one can boast.

All of our selfishness, deceit, hatred and pride, along with everything that fills the prisons of the world, were nailed to the cross. It was the ultimate act of forgiveness. Jesus paid the price for your pardon with His very life. Is it any wonder you are precious to Him? You are forgiven! However, you are free to accept or reject this great gift. He asks you to choose today whom you will serve. Jesus wept over Jerusalem as He remembered how He longed to shelter them like a mother hen shelters her brood under her wings, but they would not have it. Jesus will never force faith in Him on you, but He does ask you to choose.

Joshua 24:15

But if serving the Lord seems undesirable to you, then choose for yourselves this day whom you will serve.

Years ago, I shared the story of the cross with a class of children I was teaching. I explained the story as if my little son had done something very wrong. I told them that the judge banged His gavel and loudly pronounced, "Guilty!" Then he said "You are going to jail!" As the eyes of the children widened in fear at the thought of my son's terrible plight, I told them that I stepped forward before the judge and said, "Judge, please forgive my son. He did not know what he was doing since he is young. Please send me to jail in his place." The judge accepted my offer and my son went free. I then asked the children, "Would you like Jesus to do that for you?" They all jumped up with enthusiasm and said, "Yes!" That is what Jesus did on your behalf and mine. He paid the penalty He did not deserve, and erased the debts He did not owe. After this great sacrifice, He now stands at the door of your heart, asking if you will accept His great redeeming sacrifice for forgiveness.

Hebrews 1:1-3

In the past God spoke to our ancestors through the prophets at many times and in various ways, ² but in these last days he has spoken to us by his Son, whom he appointed heir of

all things, and through whom also he made the universe.
³ The Son is the radiance of God's glory and the exact
representation of his being, sustaining all things by his
powerful word. After he had provided purification for sins,
he sat down at the right hand of the Majesty in heaven.

When you say a sincere prayer, asking God to be Lord of your life and forgive you of all past wrongdoing, you are taking your first step of faith. In so doing, God enters via His Spirit, wipes the slate clean and gives you a fresh start. He will be there for you and will be faithful to you, even when you are faithless. You will grow in His Spirit. I have seen so many people who have taken this step of acknowledging Jesus as Lord. It is real! It changes people and sets them on a new course. I have seen the radiance of God's glory wash over the faces of those who meet God in faith. Some feel like everything looks brighter and clearer, and some shed tears of joy as the Great Spirit of Love fills their hearts. It really is a spiritual birth and truly brings you into the vibration and frequency of the Divine Spirit that is present everywhere. The loving heart of God will strengthen you and stand by you, if you allow it.

Isaiah 41:10

So do not fear, for I am with you;
do not be dismayed, for I am your God.
I will strengthen you and help you;
I will uphold you with my righteous right hand.

CLOSING THOUGHTS

We have reached the end of this book. It is my hope that you have learned something about the great heart of God who created the universe and who created you in His image. God is the Spirit and that Spirit is love, and that love is everywhere in fullness. It is the Spirit who operates within the power of energy, vibrations and frequencies. We can move up and down the levels of frequencies and vibrations through our thoughts, feelings and actions. High level vibrations are positive and will impact your life in positive ways. Low level vibrations are negative and will be of little benefit. They will repel rather than attract what you want.

You are the offspring of the mighty God who is love, so live in love. If God is love and goodness, then that is the highest level of creative energy that you can be in tune with. Remember, you have not been left on earth helpless, but are seamlessly joined to all power. The power is found in your magnificent mind, which is really the only thing that you can fully control. God created you, and you have created everything else in your life. Out of your very own thoughts, you co-create with the Spirit. So make your thoughts great. Get rid of all slander, complaining, anger, and jealousy. Let love be your guide. God wants to guide and bless you, and He will do so to the level of faith that you have.

Faith will empower you, but fear will cripple and stunt you.

Hope will keep you going and enthusiasm will pull you onward. Use your imagination and bring bold prayers, with thanksgiving, before the Throne of Grace. You have a heavenly Father who wants only your best. Let the joy of the Lord be your strength. It is the thankful person who is happy, so give thanks in all things. Be generous and it will be given back to you, pressed down and overflowing. Think, speak, act and see the best. Be grateful for what you have and more will be given to you! God's love is so beautifully expressed in the following verse:

Zephaniah 3:17 (NKJV)

The Lord your God in your midst,
The Mighty One will save;
He will rejoice over you with gladness,
He will quiet you with His love,
He will rejoice over you with singing."

The verses below are my prayer for you. It is the benediction or blessing that was spoken at the end of every service in that little Baptist Church where I found the Lord Jesus, whom I had searched for with all of my heart. It was at High Park Baptist Church in Toronto, where I found the One who loves me with an everlasting love. It was at that church where I dedicated my children to God, and where I held the Celebration of life for my dear husband, Richard, when he passed away so suddenly.

That service was led by Pastor Billy Richards of Church on the Queensway in Toronto. It is a church alive with the joy of the Lord and the forward march of faith. It is a church of love and enthusiasm that reaches throughout Toronto and into the far reaches of the world.

My prayer is that you are able to open your heart to the LORD Jesus and allow His love to lead you, guide you, and bless you. May you find a thriving Church family to support, strengthen and build you up in your newly found or searching faith.

Numbers 6:24-26 (KJV)

The LORD bless thee, and keep thee:
The Lord make his face shine upon thee,
and be gracious unto thee:
The Lord lift up his countenance upon thee,
and give thee peace.

Ephesians 6:10

Finally, be strong in the Lord and in his mighty power.

Now, turn the page and, with humble sincerity, take your first giant leap of faith and say that prayer that I said so very long ago! Please message me on Facebook and tell me of your decision and, as the Lord leads the way, we will stay in touch. Remember, YOU ARE LOVED!! And GOD LONGS TO EMPOWER YOU!

Take a step in the right direction

1. **Acknowledge** "For all have sinned and come short of the glory of God."
Romans 3:23

2. **Repent** "Repent ye therefore, and be converted, that your sins may be blotted out."
Acts 3:19

3. **Confess** "If we confess our sins He is faithful and just to forgive us our sins, and to cleanse us from all unrighteousness."
1 John 1:9

4. **Believe** "He that believeth and is baptized shall be saved; but he that believeth shall not be damned." Mark 16:16

5. **Receive** "He came unto His own, and His own received Him not. But as many as received Him, to them gave he power to become the sons of God, even to them that believe on His name."
John 1:11–12

Why not take that step now and become a child of God:

"Lord Jesus, I believe You died for my sins, and I ask your forgiveness. I receive You now as my personal Saviour and invite You, as my Lord, to manage my life from this day forward. Amen."

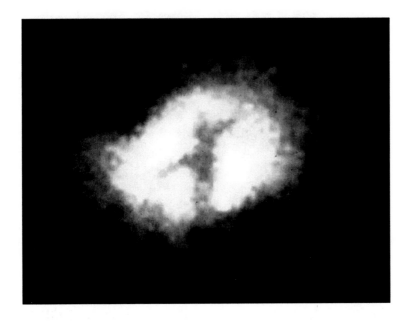

The Hubble Space Telescope found this picture, deep within the Whirlpool Galaxy! Scientists call it an "X". I would like to presume that it is the sign from the God who created the universe, which points to Jesus and the cross on which He paid the price for our pardon.

Ephesians 4:10

He who descended is the very one who ascended higher than all the heavens, in order to fill the whole universe.

Hebrews 1:1-2

God's Final Word: His Son

In the past God spoke to our ancestors through the prophets at many times and in various ways, ² but in these last days he has spoken to us by his Son, whom he appointed heir of all things, and through whom also he made the universe.

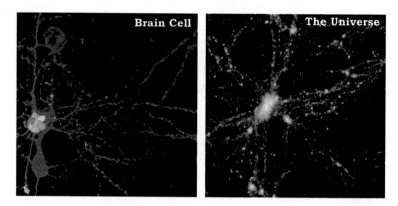

Image Source: http://www.viralnovelty.net/physicists-find-proof-universe-giant-brain/#

ABOUT THE AUTHOR

Jennifer Kiyonaga is a contributing author to the bestselling series *Empowering Women to Succeed*. She is honoured to have been included in the third book of this series which is entitled *Bounce*. Jennifer was a registered nurse for most of her career. She worked as a bedside nurse, community nurse, supervisor and Manager of Community Care.

Jennifer was a serial entrepreneur as she searched for what seemed to be calling for her. She was a Real Estate Agent, a licensed Life Insurance Agent and also held her Mutual Fund license. She thought direct sales were the answer to her search and tried many companies, but never felt fulfilled.

Her questioning heart did not settle, until she discovered that her faith is actually her purpose. Her true calling and purpose were found in the realm of spiritual writing and teaching. She wants you to know that you are loved with a supernatural love that longs to empower you and give you peace.

BIBLIOGRAPHY

Allen, James, *As a Man Thinketh*. New York, NY, Jeremy P. Tarcher/ Penguin Books, 2006.

Pressfield, Steven, *The War of Art: Break through the Blocks and Win Your Inner Creative Battles*. New York, NY, Grand Central Publishing, 2002.

Proctor, Bob, *You Were Born Rich*. Scottsdale, AZ, LifeSuccess Productions, 2002.

Spurgeon, C. H., and Robert Hall. *The Power of Prayer in a Believer's Life*. Lynnwood, WA, Emerald Books, 1993.

The Holy Bible, King James Version. Cambridge Edition: 1769; *King James Bible Online*, 2017. www.kingjamesbibleonline.org.

The Holy Bible: New American Standard Bible. 1995. LaHabra, CA: The Lockman Foundation.

The Holy Bible, New International Version. Grand Rapids, MI, Zondervan Publishing House, 1984. Used with Permission.

The Holy Bible, New King James Version. Nashville: Nelson. 1982

Wilkinson, Bruce, *The Prayer of Jabez*. Sisters, OR, Multnomah Publishers, Inc., 2001.

Wattles, Wallace, *The Science of Getting Rich.* YouTube.

The Fathers Love Letter. Used with Permission as written.

The Secret Movie. Rhonda Burn, YouTube.

15 Ways to Raise Your Vibration by Sandy Gallagher of Proctor Gallagher Institute, Arizona, USA

Other resources found on: www.youtube.com and Wikipedia and Google.